SINGING
HALLELUJAH

WHEN YOU
FEEL LIKE
HELL

SINGING
HALLELUJAH

WHEN YOU
FEEL LIKE
HELL

TIM KAUFMAN

EA Books Publishing

Published by EA Books Publishing, a division of
Living Parables of Central Florida, Inc. a 501c3
EABooksPublishing.com

ENDORSEMENTS

Tim Kaufman is a beloved recording artist who knows what "going through hell" is about. In this honest book he shares how clinical depression crushed his spirit and left him curled up in the fetal position begging for help. Through powerful stories and practical steps he walks you through tough times to find the music inside again. If you are in the pit of depression this book will guide you out, or maybe you are in a more common kind of melancholy Tim calls FTT, (*Failure to Thrive*). On either path this practical book from a trusted Christian leader will help you sing again.

Dwight Bain, Author, Leadership Coach, Media Personality
Founder, LifeWorks Group, Orlando, FL

As a concert vocalist I often open a performance by telling the audience the impact Tim Kaufman has had on my life. From giving me my first solo, as my high school music teacher, to the way he has faced and overcome the darkest times of discouragement, despair and paralyzing depression Tim's life continues to challenge and inspire me.

We live in a fallen world and will most certainly experience highs and lows, mountains and valleys, tragedies and triumphs. Having walked through many years of deep depression, here Tim tells us how he found his voice again and how God gave him a "new song" of praise. When it seems that all hell has broken loose, and the enemy has stolen our "song," there is always "one more hallelujah"! This incredible book is a must read for those struggling with any form of fear and depression and will help you find that hallelujah.

Lynda Randle, Author, Speaker, Singer, Songwriter
Founder, Lynda Randle Ministries

What could be more powerful or compelling than a testimony that takes you to a place beyond mere words? Tim's story will reveal how he found hope and yes, even songs, in the darkest times. In the pages of this book you'll learn how to worship passionately no matter where life takes you.

Dr. David Uth, Senior Pastor
First Baptist Church, Orlando, FL

Rarely has a book on depression been both informative and deeply personal. Tim has done his homework. He has gathered clinical information that is often missing within the church but then dared to offer the authentication of personal experience to the mix. For any who struggle with depression, validation, understanding, and biblical perspectives are found here.

Christine Wyrtzen, Author, Singer, Songwriter, Speaker
Founder, Daughters of Promise

Singing Hallelujah When You Feel Like Hell isn't just a book with a clever title. It is a firsthand account of someone who has been through the darkness and lived to tell about it. Tim is not just my father-in-law, he is also a wise and godly man who is willing to be vulnerable with his own story in order to reach out and minister to the many friends and loved ones we all have who deal with depression. Odds are that even if you haven't struggled with it, you love someone who has or does and they would benefit from reading this book.

Nate Claiborne, Th.M., Teacher, Book Reviewer, and
Theological Researcher, Orlando, FL

The old painting "masters," such as Rembrandt, were incredibly skilled at dramatizing a scene through the contrasts of light and darkness. In his new book, my friend Tim Kaufman, paints a powerful picture. God has allowed the darkness of depression and the shadows of despair for hope and grace to shine brighter in Tim's life and ministry. Better than most, he says, "I understand…I know the way out; follow me." Read this book—if you don't need it now, you or someone you love will need it to save a life or a ministry.

Like Tim, you can declare, "With my song I give thanks to Him; the Lord is the strength of His people" (Psalms 28:7, 8 ESV).

Dr. Hayes Wicker, Senior Pastor
First Baptist Church, Naples, FL

Tim and I served on a church staff together. We often had conversations about his depression. Why? I live with a spouse who suffers from chronic depression and anxiety disorder and I needed help understanding what she goes through. Because of his willingness to be vulnerable, this book will help not only those who suffer from depression but also those who live with someone who battles depression. It might even be life-saving.

Rev. Fred Thompson, Senior Pastor
Mt. Gilead Baptist Church, Griffin, GA

TABLE OF CONTENTS

ACKNOWLEDGMENTS

A n acknowledgement page is really a "team recognition page." You know the familiar acronym, TEAM — Together Everyone Accomplishes More. That couldn't be truer than in a book effort.

Artists Diane, Alicia, Kay, and Michelle: From conceptualization to the finished cover design, I'm amazed at your talents and insights.

Editors Kristen and John: Now I know why most of those "write your e-book in a weekend" seminars are, ummm, let's just say, "lacking." This process was rigorous and challenging. And I grew through it. Thank you for helping this rookie author.

Project Coordinator Kristen V.: Thank you for your kind accountability and keeping me on task.

Rich, Nate, Alicia: You read a book that wasn't final and I appreciate your critiques, corrections, and accountability to accuracy (a nice way of saying we're not going to let you embellish, mislead or exaggerate!).

Front Cover Design: Alicia Kaufman, Diane Vivian, Kay McConnaughey, Michelle Suazo

Back Cover Design: Diane Vivian, Creative Artistry, Winter Springs, FL

Back Cover Photo: Dan Huntting, Focus Productions, Lutz, FL

Final Edit: Debbie Huntting, Focus Productions, Lutz, FL, Steve Rogers

DEDICATION

To my frat brother, friend, and fellow-traveler *Rich*...you have and continue to "overcome." Your response to the reading of this book moved me and ministered to me. I love your heart for God and Jen.

To my frat brother and hurting friend *Warren*...it wasn't supposed to be like this was it, Ellie deciding to go to heaven ahead of us? Yet we know...we *know* that somehow, someway, all things work together for good to God's kids, even an untimely death. And I *know* as well that you will persevere through it all because Philippians 1:6 will be fulfilled in you just like it was in Ellie.

To *"Kimmo"*...when almost all was lost the Father found you. You have run well. Thanks for your comeback example. More than an excellent accompanist you are a true friend. I miss our times on the road together.

To my BFF and the wife of my youth, *Alicia*...you have persevered like so few. As much as "I love you" I admire you. Thank you for all you've done and continue to do for me, our family, and for Jesus.

To *Jesus*, my Lord, my God, my Friend and Brother...I don't deserve all You've done these many years and the last few in particular. But I'll take it, with a heart full of gratitude. Amen.

FOREWORD

When Tim Kaufman sings, people stop and listen. Not only do they worship but they are moved. On Sunday mornings, in the life group (Sunday School class) that my wife, Ruth, and I attend, we chat with the Kaufmans. Besides theology and politics Tim loves to talk all things sports. A fan of Indiana University, the Orlando Magic, and the Cincinnati Reds, conversation is never at a lull!

Tim is warm, always smiling, upbeat and (I thought) positive. I was shocked when Tim shared his story with me.

Here's a guy with a lovely and loving wife, five solid kids who are contributing to society, and a music and speaking ministry that has a track record of over forty years of excellence and fruitfulness.

I would never have guessed him to have a life-long battle with depression.

One night at dinner I peppered him with question after question: What's it feel like to be depressed for weeks or months? What's a typical day like for you? How long do your down times last? How dark does it get?

Finally he said, "Pat, I'm actually writing a book that I hope will answer all those questions and more."

I'm glad to say that book is here. Whether it's a friend, loved one or even you that feels like Tim, you will be given understanding, insight, and tools to overcome and sing hallelujah.

Pat Williams
Author, Speaker, and
Senior VP, Orlando Magic

INTRODUCTION

Some parts of our world get only about forty days of sunshine each year. Can you imagine how oppressive that must be? Gray skies, an absent sun, and usually, a cold oppressive wind afflict the body and soul.

Someone who struggles with depression, no matter the circumstances, feels this constantly. Yes, there are those rare sunny days when you can peel off an emotional coat or sweater. Some people and activities can bring an occasional smile to your face, but that gray overcast shrouds the soul. That is the constant.

You and those close to you know exactly what I'm talking about. You live with the unending sadness, hopelessness, and fears that nothing will change...ever.

But change is possible.

On Friday, January 8, 2010, at exactly 8:20 a.m., I was shaking uncontrollably. I was in the fetal position, more fearful than I had ever been—but for no apparent reason. I could only say to my wife, Alicia, "I'm so afraid. I'm so afraid."

Around 8:45 a.m., Alicia got a call from our dear friend Lorraine Mahan. "I'm in the area. Would it be OK to stop by?"

When Lorraine arrived, she took one look at me and said to Alicia, "We have to get Tim to a doctor, now!" As a pastor's wife, Lorraine has seen a great deal and knows the difference between mere sadness and depression, especially when a situation can become dangerous.

That day began a season of recovery that would be excruciating, embarrassing, and eye opening. Not to mention difficult on my family. I was at a fork in the road. If I had not begun to confront my emotional and psychological challenges right then, I might not be here now.

I'm all for the Second Amendment, but I will never have a gun in our house for this reason: if I'd had access to a firearm, I very well may have used it.

I do not share this to be melodramatic. I want to emphasize how debilitating and serious a clinical depression can be. Even for a Christian. Even for the head of a spiritually focused household. The sense of shame for someone in spiritual leadership can increase because of expectations both self-imposed and implied.

As a family, we went through the dark night of the soul. And without my family, specifically my wife, I would not have made it. I remember asking Alicia during a tender moment, "Why haven't you left me?"

She simply said, "You're my family." That one phrase—the proverbial "word fitly spoken" (Proverbs 25:11)—helped me limp on.

By the grace of the Father and His promise in Philippians 1:6, our stories (yours and mine) never end because "He who began a good work in you will be faithful to perfect it until the day of Christ Jesus." You and I are works in progress, and our war with our own minds may never be won this side of eternity. But this is an account of the tools we have been given to win the battles until the day of Christ Jesus. The outcome is assured.

But until that day, we have to understand that, with depression, there is always a root issue, and there are always lies we believe. I want you to use my story to investigate your own mind. Yes, there may be some physiological aspects to the mental struggles you face but they are certainly compounded by the experiences and relationships you have had. When we uncover those roots and confront those lies, we can begin to isolate the darkness from the light. And when we walk in the light as He is in the light, our joy is made full. That is the road we are headed down now. As we go on, consider in your heart where your own roots of bitterness may lie and ask the Lord to show you the untruths to which these roots have given life.

The tools at our disposal are many. With them you will find, as I did, that the music doesn't have to be in the minor key most of the time...that you really can sing your peaceful song (and occasionally your "happy song") again, even if at times you feel like hell.*

One final note: In the interest of privacy, I have changed the names of some of the people mentioned in this book. Whenever this happens, I have introduced them by putting their name in quotation marks.

Disclaimer: This book is not intended as a substitute for the medical advice of physicians. The reader should regularly consult a physician in matters relating to his/her health and particularly with respect to any symptoms that may require diagnosis or medical attention.

---

* See Addendum 1 for a summary on my use of the word *hell*.

SINGING
HALLELUJAH

WHEN YOU
FEEL LIKE
HELL

CHAPTER 1

AN OVERVIEW OF DEPRESSION

If you or your friend or loved one is struggling with depression, you don't need a definition to explain it. You just know it. Often, words fail to communicate what you're feeling or thinking. But a formal definition gives us a place to start the discussion and keeps us on the same page.

THE WHAT OF DEPRESSION

According to Dictionary.com, depression is "a condition of general emotional dejection and withdrawal; sadness greater and more prolonged than that warranted by any objective reason." However, what I've battled on and off for decades is a *clinical* depression, also known as Major Depressive Disorder (MDD). MDD is "a depression so severe as to be considered abnormal, either because of no obvious environmental causes, or because the reaction to unfortunate life circumstances is more intense or prolonged than would generally be expected."[1]

My personal definition is: "a dark tunnel with no light at the end of it, not even the proverbial train!"

Depression may not be a constant condition. It may go into hiding for a little while, but as a friend of mine says, "I'll be going along fine and then all of a sudden it [depression] jumps on my back, latches on, and won't let go!" And he's off to the couch again.

OK…we may know what depression *is*, but where does it come from? Why does it happen? And of course we ask, "Why is this happening to *me*?"

1

THE WHY OF DEPRESSION

WebMD.com lists at least nine primary reasons for depression including:

- **Abuse**. Past physical, sexual, or emotional abuse can increase the vulnerability to clinical depression later in life.
- **Certain medications**. Some drugs can increase your risk of depression, such as Accutane (used to treat acne), the antiviral drug interferon-alpha, and corticosteroids.
- **Conflict**. Someone with biological vulnerability may develop depression from personal conflicts or disputes with family members or friends.
- **Death or a loss**. Sadness or grief from the death or loss of a loved one, though natural, may increase the risk of depression.
- **Genetics**. A family history of depression may increase the risk. It's thought that depression is a complex trait, probably linked to multiple genes rather than just one. The genetics of depression, like most psychiatric disorders, are not as simple or straightforward as in *purely* genetic diseases such as Huntington's chorea or cystic fibrosis.
- **Major events**. Obviously negative events, like losing a job or income, can lead to depression. However, so can positive events such as starting a new job, graduating, or getting married. Any big life change, good or bad, can cause stress, but that's normal—it's not necessarily clinical depression.
- **Other personal problems**. Problems such as social isolation due to other mental illnesses or being cast out of a family or social group can contribute to the risk of clinical depression.

- **Serious illnesses**. Sometimes depression coexists with a major illness or may be triggered by another medical condition.
- **Substance abuse**. Nearly thirty percent of people with substance abuse problems also have major or clinical depression.[2]

Let me encourage you to identify which of the above are causes or contributors to your depression seasons or episodes. For me, at different times over the decades, my depressions were triggered by abuse (verbal—and not from any family member, fortunately), conflict, loss, major events, and genetics. According to my counselor and psychiatrist, the largest share of the cause, about sixty percent, was genetics.

So what about you? Can you pinpoint which of the causes are contributing to your depression? Having courage to put a name (and perhaps a face) on "what's ailin' ya" will enable you to identify and, over time, overcome your depression. And you want to overcome it, right? You wouldn't be reading this book if you weren't searching for an answer to why this dark cloud just keeps following you around.

Allow me to suggest pausing at this point and getting a journal of some sort. Look at the list above again and write down the reason or reasons that seem to be contributing to your feelings. At least take a pen and make a few notes in the margin. Later we will talk about naming names in the event of abuse or neglect by an individual.

THE WHO OF DEPRESSION

Researcher and writer for *Medical Daily*, Stephanie Castillo, identifies the people most prone to depression.[3] See if you fit one or more of the categories:

- Introverts
- Perfectionists

- Creative types (e.g. Robin Williams, Earnest Hemingway)
- Women
- Hispanics
- African Americans
- Transgender people
- Teens with family in the military
- Veterans returning from deployment
- People with no more than a high school education
- People who have been divorced
- People over forty-five

According to this list, if you are an introverted Hispanic or African American woman just returning from active military deployment who has been divorced, struggles with gender identity, has a teenage child, and is a creative perfectionist with only a G.E.D., you are on my prayer list!

Seriously, if you find yourself anywhere on this list, you are prone to battle with depression. That is not to say that people not on the list won't experience depression. It's just our raw data to better understand what we are dealing with.

Per the list, I have four strikes against me; I'm an introverted, creative perfectionist who is over forty-five. Thankfully, I've sanded down my perfectionist side quite a bit. But the introversion, age factor, and creativity remain and always will.

And that is wonderful. How God made you and me is both something to celebrate and to wrestle with. I say wrestle because your struggle is not simply against your past, your environment, your family, and the "who" of what you are; it's also against your raw humanity and sinfulness. As an ordained minister, I will discuss at length later the spiritual components of depression.

So again, take your journal and identify where you are on this list. Understand that this is simply a beginning exercise to develop a battle strategy for the long term.

DEPRESSION AS A DISEASE

Quoting Dr. Ramani Durvasula, Stephanie Castillo writes, "Depression is an illness and it is nothing to be ashamed of," Durvasula said. "You cannot 'will yourself' out of it. A person cannot be 'blamed' for being depressed any more than you can blame them for having other diseases."[4]

I really had trouble with this at first. I stigmatized myself and others who battled depression as weak-willed or undisciplined people. I would indulge in emotional self-flagellation, beating myself up for not being strong enough or tough enough. Then I'd start blaming God for not making me stronger or more capable.

But in all my reading, research, and sessions with Bob (my counselor, with over thirty-five years of professional experience), we can conclusively say that clinical depression is a disease. It is an illness. And let's call it what it is—mental illness. I'm not trying to be silly or light here, but I want you to repeat after me: "Depression is mental illness, like any other illness."

Do you know why you had trouble saying that? One word: *stigma*.

One of the problems with stigma is that it prevents people who need help from getting it. Nearly sixty percent of people who need help don't seek it for this very reason.[5]

Don't you be one of them.

Be like my dad, who suffered with three awful clinical depressions and at age eighty-eight is still taking medication. And he's been doing well for the last twenty years (thanks to a new medication)! But it wasn't always so.

A SUMMER TO FORGET

It was 1965. Gas was 31 cents a gallon, the Vietnam War was in full swing, and the Beatles released four albums. Winston Churchill died, the Dodgers won the World Series, and the Celtics beat the Lakers in the NBA finals.

And my dad was in the hospital.

I was eleven years old. I didn't know much, but I knew this wasn't the way things were supposed to be. Dad was supposed to be there in the stands for my Little League games. Mom wasn't supposed to cry, and my two sisters (another would arrive in 1967) weren't supposed to be asking, "Mommy, when will Daddy be home?"

Dad was at the V.A. hospital in Indianapolis, a two-and-a-half-hour drive from our small town of Liberty, Indiana. Once in a while, Mom would go by herself to visit Dad, but most of the time she would load up the three of us kids, and we'd head for Indy and make a "field trip" of it. I remember stopping for fast food on the way up and back, counting cows with my sisters to help make the trip go faster, and reading a *Sports Illustrated* when we couldn't find any more cows. I remember just being together at a picnic table not far from Dad's quarters, talking, eating, and trying to be "normal" as a family. Then darkness started to descend, interrupting it all. The two-plus-hour drive home always seemed longer than the first drive. Probably because we couldn't see any cows.

For me, one day Dad was going to work and the next, he couldn't get out of bed. He stayed in bed for several days, and after Grandpa couldn't pep-talk him out of it, off to the hospital he went. Dad stayed for eight long months.

Looking back, one would think that my grandfather would have understood better. After all, he'd had two depressions himself.

Hmmm...Grandpa had two depressions, Dad three, and three for me too. Hence the question:

IS THERE A GENETIC CONNECTION TO DEPRESSION?

To answer this, I simply want to refer you to a study published in the *American Journal of Psychiatry*, conducted by Drs. Patrick F. Sullivan, Michael C. Neale, and Kenneth S. Kendler in October of 2000. Here are their summary conclusions:

Major depression is a familial disorder, and its familiality mostly or entirely results from genetic influences. Environmental influences specific to an individual are also etiologically significant. Major depression is a complex disorder that does not result from either genetic or environmental influences alone but rather from both. These findings are notably consistent across samples and methods and are likely to be generally applicable.[6]

Simply put, upbringing may help genetics along. You may have the genetic disposition for depression, and then one or both parents will model the behavior of a depressive. So you may get the "advantage" of learning how to "do depression" well. You imitate what you see, and your genetic map strengthens this behavior.

A telling example was related to me by my wife, Alicia. Early in our marriage when I would phone home for whatever reason, she would notice that my voice inflections would change. My conversation cadence would slow, a somber mood would take over the conversation and by the time I would hang up she would wonder, "Who is the person I just heard talking on the phone?" As I began to take note I had to confess at times I sounded like the Disney character Eeyore!

One advantage to knowing our family of origin interplay is in how to approach a treatment plan. When my psychiatrist found out that my dad and grandfather were depressives, he asked, "Do you know what medicine your father is currently taking?" and, "How is he doing with that medication?"

An immediate phone call went to Indiana. I learned what Dad was taking (and enjoying success with). So my doctor prescribed a similar medication for me. He also added a second medication. After about a month or so, the cloud began to lift, though I still had a long way to go due to other factors (which we will discuss as we progress through the book).

I am still on both meds today (both at half the dose I was taking in 2010), and plan on being on them for life if necessary.

Another advantage awareness of the genetic component is how this can help family members cope. While my wonderful wife, Alicia, cannot truly understand depression, she accepts it and helps me navigate the reality of it.

FAMILY HELP

After my crash and burn in January of 2010, one of the most thoughtful things Alicia did was to schedule a therapeutic massage for me. It did several things:

- It was a welcome distraction (for both of us).
- It was medicinal, both physically and emotionally.
- It got me out of bed, moving, and out of the house.
- It gave her a ninety-minute care-giving break.
- It gave us something new to talk about.
- Since we were out, we did some other things (thus extending the day).

The most important thing is, we did *something*!

I remember hearing Dr. Charles Stanley on his *In Touch* radio broadcast preaching on emotional health and him saying, "If you are battling depression, the first thing you must do is *do something, anything!*"

Like Dr. Stanley, I want to encourage you to do something: take a walk, go to the mall, work out at the gym, visit a counselor, watch a movie, read a book. And if you are a friend or loved one of the depressed, do something with him or her. Do something that will begin the process of healing, even if it seems insignificant.

Because it isn't.

Any constructive activity with one or more people is a step toward wholeness, toward normality. With the right combination of medicine, cognitive therapy (how we think and interpret life and its events), good people, and correct spiritual resources, we can get better.

So, let's summarize:

- Depression is real.
- Depression has causes.
- Depression is a disease.
- Depression has solutions.

Part of getting better is understanding our past.

CHAPTER 2

FAMILY HISTORY

N ature vs. nurture—we have studied it in Psychology 101, read about it in parenting books, and seen it in action through society. We have experienced it. Some individuals are genetically predisposed to mental disorders.

I have a serotonin deficiency that runs in my family. This makes mood regulation difficult. That's nature. Depending on the nurture, it is possible to have this type of challenge and it not fall into a lifelong pattern of misery and unrest. However, that was not my story.

SEROTONIN

But first a word about serotonin. You may have heard the term and know it relates to mental health. However, many are unclear on what exactly it is and how it comes to bear on your emotional makeup.

Serotonin is defined as: "a neurotransmitter, derived from tryptophan, which is involved in sleep, depression, memory, and other neurological processes."[7]

OK…but what's a neurotransmitter?

I don't want to get too technical here, but suffice it to say that:

Neurotransmitters are the brain chemicals that communicate information throughout our brain and body. They relay signals between nerve cells, called 'neurons.' The brain uses neurotransmitters to tell your heart to beat, your lungs to breathe, and your stomach to digest. They can also affect mood, sleep, concentration, weight, and can cause adverse symptoms when they are out of balance. Neurotransmitter levels can be depleted many ways. As a matter of fact, it is estimated that eighty-six percent of Americans have suboptimal neurotransmitter levels.

Stress, poor diet, neurotoxins, genetic predisposition, drugs (prescription and recreational), alcohol and caffeine usage can cause these levels to be out of optimal range...there are two kinds of neurotransmitters – Inhibitory and Excitatory. Excitatory neurotransmitters are not necessarily exciting – they are what stimulate the brain. Those that calm the brain and help create balance are called inhibitory. Inhibitory neurotransmitters balance mood and are easily depleted when the excitatory neurotransmitters are overactive.[8]

SPECIFICALLY...

Serotonin is an inhibitory neurotransmitter – which means that it does not stimulate the brain. Adequate amounts of serotonin are necessary for a stable mood and to balance any excessive excitatory (stimulating) neurotransmitter firing in the brain. If you use stimulant medications or caffeine in your daily regimen – it can cause a depletion of serotonin over time. Serotonin also regulates many other processes such as carbohydrate cravings, sleep cycle, pain control and appropriate digestion. Low serotonin levels are also associated with decreased immune system function.[9]

Wow! When I first learned how important serotonin levels were to our overall health, as well as how many factors can affect those levels, I immediately started taking the medication that my doctor advised.

Plus, I made some dietary changes. Over the years as a traveling musician and presenter, I've consumed more coffee than I'd like to admit. (You name the brand, I can tell you if it's good, better or best!) And to think that this may have been contributing to my depletion of serotonin all the time. What we don't know *can* kill us.

But what about your family history? What about my family history? What was it in our nurturing years that happened (or didn't happen or should have happened) that affected how we saw (and maybe still see) the world? What did our early life experiences teach us about authority, emotional safety, friendships, trust, and risk? Who were the people (family, friends, teachers, etc.) that influenced us for the good or bad?

"NOT GOOD ENOUGH, NEVER HAVE ENOUGH"

I'm not sure exactly when it started, but most of my life, I have heard a tape playing in my head: "Not good enough, never have enough; not good enough, never have enough." Over and over this would loop—sometimes loud, other times barely audible background noise—but playing nonetheless. The tune was haunting; the lyrics, defining.

In 1991, during my third therapy session, the counselor told me that during prayer we would ask the Holy Spirit to show me whom I needed to forgive and of whom I needed to ask forgiveness. Hebrews 12:15 speaks of "roots of bitterness" that take hold inside and affect our relationships. Our aim was to discover my roots of bitterness.

As most of you know, basketball in Indiana is a cultural obsession. Actually, that's a bit of an understatement. The Gene Hackman movie *Hoosiers*, gives you some idea what "Hoosier Hysteria" is like. And it can be intimidating if you aspire to play the game but don't measure up. Compound that with the fact that your father is the most successful basketball player from the county—someone who won a sectional tournament, set scoring records, and became a scholarship player at (where else?) Indiana University.

Me? Having started school in another county, I was a year younger than all my classmates. Though one year hardly makes any difference for adults, sixth versus seventh grade seems diametric. In pick-up games, I was always the last or next-to-last choice. They avoided me in the offensive plays. If I shot the ball, it was by accident. I was not "good enough."

My dad's shadow loomed over me, imposed by coaches, parents of classmates, and myself (never my dad). I became

13

convinced I would never be good enough. It just was not possible. "Not good enough" was always playing, and the recording just kept getting louder.

Again, I am not sure where the seed came from, but plenty of water, fertilizer, and cultivation came from my sixth grade teacher, "Mr. Prichard." I want to think he meant well. I try to imagine what demons he was fighting. His private battles spilled out all over a number of us in his class. One particular friend and I always seemed to make his hit list. Mr. Prichard deftly used shame as his tool to "instill aspirations of higher education excellence" in his students.

Do you remember being called up to the board to solve an equation in front of the entire class? For good students, it simply reinforced what everyone already knew: they were always right. For those of us who struggled, it also reinforced what everyone already knew: we were always wrong. It was public humiliation. I am not saying this method of teaching is wrong, but apparently some teachers in the sixties didn't understand that many students had different ways of learning. There is a difference between constructive criticism and abrasive speech that can be harmful.

One day Mr. Prichard sent eight of us to the board to do a math problem. As usual, seven would finish and take their seats while I remained up front still wondering how to begin.

That day, Mr. Prichard had a brilliant idea to help his wayward student. He called the office to send down my sister from her third grade class to assist me. He wanted me to see how simple it was. With some coaching from him and one of our A+ students, my sister successfully solved the problem.

Of course, I, along with a couple other "cool" guys, laughed it off. Inside, though, all I could hear was that tape reminding me, "You will never be good enough." It droned so loud, I was sure someone else would notice.

The sense of shame was overwhelming. The laughter and stories that circulated around Liberty Elementary School for the next few days were devastating to this sensitive, artistic kid. I just wanted people to like me, accept me, and think well of me. They made fun of me on the playground, in the lunchroom, and anywhere else on the school campus. I felt trapped by the shame and embarrassment.

From that day on, I was marked. Since I was officially the math dunce, I gave up trying. This was not a conscious decision or an act of rebellion. I genuinely believed that I would never succeed, so why try? I got Cs and Ds in math and the sciences all through my ensuing years.

On the midterm Algebra II exam during my junior year, I got a thirty-six percent. So how did I pass with a D minus? That's easy. Because my math teacher also happened to be the baseball coach, and I was the number one pitcher on the team! I transferred to Business Math, which was really a free pass if you weren't going to college and just needed a math credit to get out of high school. Finally, I was good enough—for basic remedial math!

During my recounting the story to my counselor ("Jill"), I became extremely agitated, and she asked me why I was shaking so much. The truth was that I very much wanted to go back in time and cause my teacher some serious physical pain! Though Jill empathized, she made it clear that my teacher was the one I needed to forgive that day; he was one of my roots of bitterness.

It was not at all easy, but I did verbalize forgiveness for him that day. She explained that the feelings of pity and understanding would follow eventually as I continued to choose forgiveness. It was a beginning step toward better mental health.

Would you pause right now and consider…do you have one or two moments that you feel defined you as a person? As painful as it might be, reenter the situation and see and feel the injustice. Acknowledge the absolute wrong. Then… choose to forgive.

This is one of the differences between secular and Christian counseling. We go back not to find someone to blame but to find someone to forgive. For some of you, that may be a long process. But I know it's possible because there are people who have extended forgiveness to the worst of the worst.

A most powerful story is about Dutch evangelist Corrie Ten Boom and her family. In 1944, they had been actively rescuing Jews from the Nazis when a fellow Dutch citizen betrayed them. Her father died after ten days in prison, and her sister Betsy died near the end of the ten months. If anyone had a "right" to be bitter, it was Corrie.

But then the Lord confronted her with a challenge few ever face: forgive your persecutor. Corrie relates it:

It was at a church service in Munich that I saw him, the former SS man who had stood guard at the shower room door in the processing center at Ravensbruck. He was the first of our actual jailers that I had seen since that time. And suddenly it was all there – the roomful of mocking men, the heaps of clothing, Betsie's pain-blanched face.

He came up to me as the church was emptying, beaming and bowing. "How grateful I am for your message, Fraulein," he said. "To think that, as you say, He has washed my sins away."

His hand was thrust out to shake mine. And I, who had preached so often to the people in Bloemendaal the need to forgive, kept my hand at my side. Even as the angry, vengeful thoughts boiled through me, I saw the sin of them. Jesus Christ had died for this man; was I going to ask for more? "Lord Jesus, I prayed, "forgive me and help me to forgive him."

I tried to smile, and I struggled to raise my hand. I could not. I felt nothing, not the slightest spark of warmth or charity. And so again I breathed a silent prayer. "Jesus, I cannot forgive him. Give me Your forgiveness."

As I took his hand, the most incredible thing happened. From my shoulder and along my arm and through my hand a current seemed to pass from me to him while into my heart sprang a love for this stranger that almost overwhelmed me.

And I discovered that it is not on our forgiveness any more than on our goodness that the world's healing hinges, but on His. When He tells us to love our enemies, He gives, along with the command, the love itself.[10]

It wasn't until I forgave Mr. Prichard in Jill's counseling office that I began to be free of this defining event in my life.

As I suggested in the introduction, you cannot put your finger on one childhood mental wound and move on with a clean and peaceful psyche. Many experiences affect and mold your self-image and how you make decisions based on that. Though I believe the wounds Mr. Prichard inflicted on my soul were catalysts, other experiences reinforced the "not-good-enough" script that framed my life.

Again, take a moment to journal or list some events that have come to mind as you've read this chapter. Recall and write down names, incidents, or painful memories that have marked you and your very soul. Then share these with a trusted friend or counselor and allow that person to challenge you to take on the issue. If it involves having to extend forgiveness, go there. Start the healing process.

TURNING POINT

One of the revelations that was surprising at first but later made so much sense is how much one single perspective contributed to my depression, in a major way. I believe that it was the turning point of my healing. Perhaps in the most powerful and consequential way.

I was reminded the other day of how powerful our parents seek from them. Our one-year-old granddaughter Piper is learning to walk with her little walker and doing quite well. I was helping her, getting her course-corrected or restarted and following her. Every few steps she would look at me, to see if I was watching. It was as if she was saying, "Poppy, do you see me? Do you think I am doing well? Do you like what I'm doing?"

This repeated itself, over and over again. Of course, I was loving it!

We grow through childhood, adolescence, and young adulthood wanting and needing the applause and encouragement of our parent(s) and significant people in our lives.

There comes a day however, when every one of us has to cut the cord of emotional dependency. We have to walk life out on our own and emotionally "leave" our family of origin and create a new family. We have to understand that we were made differently and are called by God to carve out a unique place in His economy of life. God is very intentional about this as He gives specific instruction to the first couple in history, Adam and Eve.

LEAVE AND CLEAVE

Therefore shall a man leave his father and his mother, and shall cleave unto his wife: and they shall be one flesh (Genesis 2:24 KJV).

One of the major reasons for marital and familial conflict is the failure of a husband or wife (but mostly the husband) to "leave" their family of origin, and to "cleave" ("join to," "bond with," "hold fast to," "unite to") to each other in every way, especially emotionally. I say mostly the husband because God has given to him the charge and calling to lead the home and to love his wife "just as Christ loved the Church and gave Himself up for her" (Ephesians 5:25).

How many couples have, in a counseling session, blurted out something like…

- Wife: "That sounds like your father talking," or
- Husband: "Why do we always have to go to your mother's house? Can't we do something just the two of us?" or
- Wife: "You love your mother more than me!"
- Husband: "I'm not your dad; I don't do things like your dad and never will!"

Here was the rub for me: As I've shared, I was always feeling like I was on the verge of failure in many of the things I would attempt, but the *one thing* I knew I had done right was marrying Alicia. How we met, how the Lord arranged for us to not be separated geographically in 1980, (the year we fell in love), how I *finally* found my soul-mate and followed through, without fear, to marry her. After getting engaged to two other great people and bailing both times — yeah, I'm that guy, and there's a complicated story here too, for another time — I had gotten *this* right, for sure.

PAUSE

I want to share some things frankly that I know will help you, friend. In doing so it may seem that I'm throwing some of the members of my family under the bus. Nothing could be further from the truth. We've come to terms with our issues (as a friend of mine likes to say, "You've got issues; I've got issues; all God's children have issues!") and if high-profile pastor Andy Stanley can talk about the divorce of his high-profile mother and pastor-father, Dr. Charles Stanley, and extrapolate life-lessons from sharing, I know our story can help you and others too. I'm grateful for family members who are committed to growing in their relationship with Christ and owning their issues and working through them as best they can. That's really all one can ask of another loved one.

RESUME

My family of origin was hardly approving of my selection of a wife, especially my father (from whom other family members took their cue) who had a subconscious dislike for strong women. I had heard it all my life. Dad would say about different girls I would date or bring home:

- "You'd better not let her put a ring in your nose" or
- "She's yanking your chain buddy" or
- "You don't want to be hen-pecked with her now do you?"

...and other unspoken body language signals that sent the disapproval vibes loud and clear. Dad would also talk about strong women in our church in a disapproving way. He'd speak of their husbands as hen-pecked and the subconscious messaging was, "do *not* date or marry a strong woman."

As the broken record "not good enough, never have enough" played over and over again in my head it caused me to live in pretense around my parents. I have always been proud of Alicia and eager to introduce her to old friends, acquaintances, ministers, etc. In fact because of her likeable personality she has opened critical doors for me vocationally with her "WOO" (Winning Others Over) strength.[11] Her input has been invaluable to me in making many important decisions. Her positivity has been a true gift for a depressive like me. She's exactly what I needed in my life. I have been excited and proud to have her by my side.

Sadly, whenever we were around my parents, I walked on eggshells. I mistreated her and deeply wounded her. I was afraid that my dad would interpret her gifts incorrectly and disapprove of me. When she would speak, I would kick her under the table. I wouldn't sit beside her on the sofa or show her affection. As a husband who was supposed to meet her needs I wasn't generous. I would withhold.

Leading up to our thirtieth wedding anniversary, Alicia and I talked a lot about going on a cruise. It was something that I wanted to do, too. One day, in the midst of one of the most broke times in our lives financially, I had several hundred dollars in a drawer. I called her over to me and pulled out the drawer and said, "This is what I have set aside for our cruise." She was so happy. On Christmas day, we looked online together and chose the perfect cruise for our anniversary. I agreed to get it booked. As the time of the cruise grew near, Alicia asked me about the booking. I had procrastinated and neglected to book it. When we went online, it was sold out. Alicia was more than crushed. This came on the heels of twelve months of hell with me. During this period, I had spent time lying in bed in a fetal position, being AWOL in helping move out of our legacy dream home into a rental. I had been lying on the couch when we needed grocery money, and not fulfilling the commitment of taking care of our then twelve-year-old. All this while Alicia was out working to build a business, put food on the table, and pay our rent, insurance, car payments, and the rest of our monthly bills. She was more than devastated. She was furious. She was done.

She decided that she would live in the house with me but as far as she was concerned, we didn't have a relationship. She picked up the phone and called my counselor. She went to see him and vented. After seeing me/us for six months of weekly visits in his office, he had a revelation. He told her that he was praying for us that morning and asked the Holy Spirit to reveal to him the root of my depression. It hit him. The whole story about the cruise and the sabotaging of it was the trigger for him to see clearly. He shared with Alicia, "Because of Tim's constant seeking of approval from his dad he has been sinning against his conscience and not loving his wife as promised in the marriage ceremony. He has been 'loving approval' more than 'loving Alicia.'"

Miraculously, a room opened on the cruise. Before leaving, I wrote a letter to my parents detailing my sin of choosing them over Alicia, made a similar confession to our kids, and left for our thirtieth anniversary cruise. It was the best time Alicia and I ever had together as a couple. It was the honeymoon that we never had. It was her and me and no voices of disapproval.

I had tried to tactfully approach the issue with my dad after a couple of family blow ups regarding Alicia. My dad and I had a chance to talk frankly about what I believe was *his* root of bitterness issue.

Dad had been emotionally yanked around by his own mother. He was an only child and since my grandfather was a strong man, Grandma couldn't control him, but she could manipulate her son early on. And that pattern continued until she went to heaven.

I said to Dad, "I don't think your issue is with Alicia. I think it's with Grandma. She wanted to control Grandpa, but couldn't, so she resorted to controlling you."

Dad looked straight ahead, thought long and hard and finally replied, "You may have something there, Timothy." He went to bed thinking...thinking...

Even though this seemed like a breakthrough, lifelong patterns are hard to break. Dad continued to wrestle with his negative feelings for my wife and I continued to wrestle to gain his approval, all to no avail.

I was in violation of God's instruction for me to *leave* my father and mother (including their blessing for my decision to marry whom I married) and to *cleave* to my wife, without holding back any of my love or commitment to her.

Even though I had married the right person, I was not *fully* married to the right person. And it was another failure that further reinforced "not good enough."

Nature and nurture, biology and history—we need to address both correctly. Doctors can help us with the nature.

Counselors can help us with the nurture issues. A balanced treatment plan will usually include both approaches. Find out what works best for you or your loved one.

CHAPTER 3

FACING FAILURE

"Whoever said, 'It's not whether you win
or lose that counts,' probably lost."
– Martina Navratilova

H ave you ever failed? I mean, have you ever had a real humdinger of a life flameout where you hurt people and changed your life forever?

If so, welcome to the land of the living. We all have and we are in good company:

- Henry Ford, Walt Disney, and Milton Hershey went bankrupt.
- Samson was a serial adulterer (yet joined God's "Hall of Faith" in Hebrews 11).
- King David was an adulterer and murderer (yet still "a man after God's own heart" [Acts 13:22]).
- Jacob was the quintessential deceiver, yet fathered the nation of Israel.
- Joseph endured setback after setback on his way to becoming prime minister of Egypt.
- And so on…

All of these eventually overcame their setbacks.

And so can you.

We are wired to win. We just are. But in the Garden (of Eden) when we sinned, that wiring got muddled. Now we really have a talent for messing up life.

I've sung at a lot of weddings. I've officiated several. I've talked with many grooms and brides, and I've never heard one of them say something like, "Yeah, we're getting married today, but in four years I think we'll go ahead and get a divorce." No one plans that.

Your intention and mine, at whatever we do, is to score a win.

- A guy and gal go on a date. They both want it to be a good experience. Neither of them says, "I'm going to see how I can mess this up right from the start!" But it happens all too often.
- A ballplayer goes into the game with the intention of winning, not losing (unless he plays for the 76ers!). But if he makes an error or drops a pass, all he sees in the mirror is a big L.
- A student studies hard for an exam to at least pass, if not get a top grade. She pulls an all-nighter, takes the test, and feels pretty confident. Yet still she gets an F.
- A worker takes a job with the intention of becoming valuable to the boss and earning the respect of his coworkers. Then he fails to meet expectations.
- You select your career with the goal of succeeding financially and retiring comfortably after four decades or longer. Then a severe recession like 2008 destroys your plans.

Unfortunately, most of us know our share of failure. We didn't plan to fail. Frankly, we never even considered it an option.

Even when facing impossible odds, we expect to be the exception to the rule. This phenomenon is common in young men aged eighteen to twenty-six. It's why their insurance rates are high and why they make great soldiers. "The other guy's gonna die, not me." Here's a prime example:

In the fall of 1971, I was a freshman at Ball State University (BSU) in Muncie, Indiana. At our dormitory orientation, the dorm supervisor spoke to us, a group of about 120. "Take a look at the guy next to you. Next semester, one of you will be gone."

You know what every single one of us believed? "It may be him, but it won't be me." I know because my roommate and I talked about it later. Guess what?

A week later, I was a college dropout. Unforeseen circumstances back home caused one of my first life crises. Providentially, the Lord arranged for me to learn about the Christian college I would attend for the next three years on the very day I dropped out of Ball State. But sitting in that dorm lounge looking at the guy next to me, I was certain I'd stay at BSU through graduation.

We are often too sure of ourselves, especially when we are young.

I recovered from that early failure at BSU, but another would happen just a few years later. It would negatively affect the trajectory of my mental health for too long.

DEPRESSION #1

In 1977, I was a college graduate in search of professional meaning and significance. I wanted to have an itinerant gospel music career—to sing, write, record, and travel. But I "sacrificed" that dream because I (erroneously) believed God wanted me to give it all up and become a cross-cultural missionary. With well-intentioned help from friends, colleagues, and mentors, I succeeded at becoming just that.

And I lasted all of eleven months on the field.

What I should have done instead was take the counsel of my pastor, Dr. R. Herbert Fitzpatrick. He told me, "Tim, I don't know about this Portugal thing. I really think you should consider being a gospel singer here in America."

That was exactly what I wanted to do, but:

- It was more "noble" to go to the mission field (so I thought).
- It was more Christian to sacrifice what I wanted (so I thought).

- It wouldn't look good if I started in one direction and then had to admit I was wrong or didn't know how to discern God's will. (Hmmm...pride?)

So, I decided to help God out. I would manufacture God's will. What happened? I went to the Bible to get my answers — my *self-imposed* answers.

Low self-esteem, coupled with misapplied theological truth, can be a recipe for emotional and professional disaster. So hungry was I for significance that I would actually give up what God crafted me to do. I would "forsake all" and go in a ministry direction for which I was not emotionally prepared. My I.Q. was fine, but my E.Q. — my "Emotional Quotient" — was flawed.

So in my devotional time (See how spiritual I was?), I found just what I was looking for: *"Behold, thou shalt call a **nation** that thou knowest not, and **nations** that knew not thee shall run unto thee because of the Lord thy God..."* (Isaiah 55:5a KJV, emphasis mine). My "interpretation" was, "Oh, I'm supposed to go to a *nation* I've never been to, and after I'm established in that nation, I'll sing and minister in other *nations* as well!"

A few weeks later, I was wavering in my commitment about going overseas. We can't have that now! So I laid out a "fleece."[12] I said, "Lord, I need something to go on. What do You have to say?"

A day later I read in my devotions, *"And Jesus said unto him, 'No man, having put his hand to the plow, and looking back, is fit for the kingdom of God.'"* (Luke 9:62, KJV). Again, my "interpretation" was, "Wow! I started this direction and I can't go back now. I have to forge on. If not, I won't be fit for the kingdom." (Once again, I would be "not good enough!")

And forge on I did! I raised my support in record time, secured a significant overage of funds for our national account, learned Portuguese in seven months, started a mixed vocal ensemble, recorded one solo and one ensemble album, and leaped tall buildings in a single bound!

In all of that frenzied "spiritual" activity, I remained discouraged. I wondered if I was in the "right place" doing the "right things." Subliminally I was plotting my escape.

As I became quietly angry at God, I began to indulge in illicit behavior and substance abuse. Then I heard loud and clear: "Not good enough!"

I couldn't agree more, so I swore a team member to secrecy, cleaned out my bank account in Lisbon, bought a plane ticket and went home—defeated, ashamed, and very definitely "not good enough."

After two weeks in Indiana, I ended up in Maryland in the home of my childhood pastor and eventual mentor, "Pastor Fitz," and his wife, Lois. I shared with them how I had (reluctantly) led a person to the Lord on my flight.

He laughed. "Way to go, Jonah!" It was a wise and patient laugh. He somehow knew where this was headed.

I started counseling in the next few weeks—terrible counseling. It was legalistic and behavior oriented ("Stop sinning and you'll feel better"); it did next to nothing to prevent a depression that lasted almost a year.

It also didn't help that well-intentioned people were saying stuff like, "Tim will never be happy until he returns to Portugal. He learned the language so quickly. The music ministry was flourishing under his leadership." And so on.

I would hear this chatter secondhand, and it would only cause me more despair. It seemed I truly was Jonah, having gone AWOL on the first mission assignment in my life.

The depression dissipated over that year thanks to several things:

- I was in a safe place, receiving needed love and acceptance as a fallen, wounded soldier in the King's army.
- I found purpose and meaning as I worked on the church and school staff with other like-minded, on-mission people. Singing as a volunteer at a local nursing home was therapeutic as well.

- After some time away from my Bible, I read it with new eyes. It became precious again.
- I met the young lady who would become my wife, my companion, and my closest friend. She knew all about me and accepted me and loved me anyway.

I want to close this chapter with some takeaways. Overcoming our depression episodes will require several components:[13]

1. **Key People**. I mentioned my spiritual advisor, my pastor, and his wife. They provided not only wisdom but also a home for eight months. They had seen depression before. The pastor had experienced it himself. I had the space I needed either to be alone or with people who didn't judge me. What a gift.
2. **Purpose and Meaning**. I worked with a team of church and school staff who provided needed fellowship. We also had a mission together and made a difference in people's lives. The more I could serve and experience fruitfulness, the less I thought about myself and my circumstances.
3. **Life Goal**. When I met and married Alicia, life began all over again for me. As Scripture teaches, she completed me. (And guys, we need to face it—the Bible never says we complete the woman.) I felt a measure of wholeness as never before. We had the same mission in our hearts and minds—to have God's will in our lives no matter what. We were intent on pursuing that together, either until death or Jesus' return.

Finally, I want to address the issue of "manufacturing God's will" (i.e., convincing yourself that your will is God's). We find God's will

1. through His Word, the Bible.
2. through prayer.
3. through circumstances.

4. through wise counsel.
5. through steps of faith.

How had I initially misjudged God's will? It was not in depending on His Word but in *misapplying that Word* to something I had already decided to do. In hindsight, I wasn't honestly seeking. I was coming up with something that looked good and noble on the surface but was really nothing more than self-applause.

How many people do you know who have done something like this? They've made a decision and then looked for some outside validation to support that decision—no matter how unwise, harmful, or downright unbiblical. In my case, it hurt a number of people and permanently damaged some relationships. Yes, we believe in forgiveness, but you can't eliminate memories and other consequences.

Then I was also ignoring that the Bible *also* says, *"Where there is no counsel, the people fall; But in the **multitude of counselors** there is safety"* (Proverbs 11:14, NKJV, emphasis mine).

I limited the counsel I sought, looking almost exclusively within the organization I served. I should have sought out additional unbiased counsel from others like Pastor Fitz.

While I genuinely believe my organizational leaders and friends had my best interest at heart, their perspective was limited. They didn't understand my psychological and emotional dysfunction. Not to mention, they wanted to keep me around for my voice and the positive qualities I had that benefited them. This is understandable, so we need outside help in discerning God's will through a multitude of counselors.

We do not become Christ followers or earn more favor with God by what we do. Our coming to Jesus and growing in Him is a work of the Holy Spirit. The Bible says: *"For it is [not your strength, but it is] God who is effectively at work in you, both to will and to work [that is, strengthening, energizing, and creating in you the longing and the ability to fulfill your purpose]*

31

for His good pleasure" (Philippians 2:13, AMP). I experience this divine enablement when I am most submitted to Him.

> *Let me put this question to you: How did your new life begin? Was it by working your heads off to please God? Or was it by responding to God's Message to you? Are you going to continue this craziness? For only crazy people would think they could complete by their own efforts what was begun by God. If you weren't smart enough or strong enough to begin it, how do you suppose you could perfect it? Did you go through this whole painful learning process for nothing? It is not yet a total loss, but it certainly will be if you keep this up! (The apostle Paul in Galatians 3:3, The Message).*

My first depression was a combination of (very) low self-esteem, real guilt (through disobedience and hurting others), false guilt (self-condemnation and "not good enough"), unwise decisions, and a misapplication of biblical truth.

But God had a purpose. He always has a purpose.

CHAPTER 4

GREAT EXPECTATIONS AND DISAPPOINTMENT WITH GOD

"We were promised sufferings. They were part of the program.
We were even told, 'Blessed are they that mourn,' and I accept it."
—C. S. Lewis, *A Grief Observed*

Was there ever a time in your life when you knew—I mean, just *knew*—a certain thing would happen? You may not have been sure of the details, but things overall would certainly fall into your favor.

- You may have had a failure or two, but *this* time, it's all going to work out as it should. You've prayed about it along with friends and family—and God answers prayers, right?
- You aced the interview, and *this* is the job you've worked and waited for all your life. It's in the bag!
- You have been a faithful employee for over a decade, and *this* promotion has your name on it. You know you will advance to a place of financial stability and professional fulfillment.
- You're tired of the dating scene, but a friend talks you into one more blind date. And suddenly you've met the person you've been waiting for all your life! It will be a marriage made in heaven, right?
- The doctor gave you the worst news possible. But you have the church praying, and last year when they prayed for Mr. Smith, he experienced wonderful healing. You love the Lord just like Mr. Smith, and you are *sure* that God will answer their prayers again—just as He did for the Smiths.

I stiff-armed my second depression for over a decade. Marriage, kids, moving to Florida, and a full calendar of singing gigs — foreign and domestic — helped me stay busy. I didn't really have to face the pains I had buried deep inside myself. Our loving Lord would soon address those long-lost wounds.

Beginning in 1985, I appeared regularly on Dr. Charles Stanley's *In Touch* TV broadcast from Atlanta's First Baptist Church. I would sing two songs in the first service and then two different songs in the second service. Then the producers could have four songs "in the can" for four different broadcasts, whether or not I was present. I would be on the broadcast at least once a month for several years.

Finally! I thought I was coming to the end of my quest to be "good enough."

Confirmation came with a recording contract in the summer of 1990. Per the written agreement, I would record the first of three albums in March or April of 1991 and launch the album in July at the annual Christian Booksellers Association (CBA) convention at Denver! The company rented booth space at the annual GMA (Gospel Music Association) convention in Nashville that spring. There I was, hobnobbing with artists like Phil Driscoll, Dick and Mel Tunney, Larnelle Harris, and Sandi Patti.

At last I had signed with a recording company that would promote my music and ministry so I wouldn't have to. My life's goal was coming true. The implication? I was finally "good enough" and would "have enough." Life, it appeared, was good — and would be for quite some time.

My producer/arranger was none other than Lari Goss, one of the best in all of gospel music. He had arranged for many of the top singers and groups including the Gaither Vocal Band and the Brooklyn Tabernacle Choir. And what an experience it was working with Lari and his crew! We got to make decisions based on creative aspects of the song or arrangement. Budget was never a constraint.

I had also spent several nights writing or co-writing three original songs which would give the album a flair of uniqueness. My voice was at its prime. After months of arranging, recording, and mixing, we had a product called *Give Your Heart a Home*. I'm still marketing and singing several of the songs today.

But in case it sounds like an overnight success, it wasn't. In June 1991, the recording company's owner flew to Orlando, took me to lunch, and explained that he had gone bankrupt! He would have to scrap the entire project. We would arrange a long-term buyout plan so that I could have the album master, but disappointment struck hard.

I sighed and looked across the table. "Don't worry about it. It just seems to be in keeping with what God is doing in my life these days." I had a sense of resignation and fatalism. In keeping with my incomplete theological framework, I still wasn't "good enough" and needed more character refinement. I viewed God as the ultimate drill sergeant, breaking down His troops to get them ready for battle. Only after you've experienced "enough" disappointment, pain, and humiliation (rather than humility) are you "ready" for the big things God had in store for you.

God is the One who tests our hearts, and He does arrange events for our growth. He often uses pain as a catalyst, but when you see this as His only method, He becomes little more than a divine bully. You no longer see Him as the loving Father He is.

Hit with yet another loss in a series of crippling losses, I spent the next three weeks in a spiritual and emotional stupor — weeping and unable to speak. Why would God offer me a carrot of success and then yank it back like that? Wasn't I just about to do what He had gifted and built me to do?

Apparently not. I had never felt more abandoned, directionless, and disillusioned. God had let me down! One day I would be angry with Him. The next, I would retreat completely. I wanted nothing to do with Him. *He* was the one who let all this happen. My default thought: "Why in the world would You jerk me around like this?"

But did you notice? Even while I despised Him, I spoke directly to Him. At our cores we truly long for Him.

Desperate for answers, I'd go to familiar passages like Psalms 37:4: *"Delight yourself in the Lord and He will give you the desires of your heart."* Message? I must not be delighting or else I'd have the desire of my heart, a recording contract, and an expanded ministry. (Translation: "Not good enough, never have enough.")

Or my life verse, Matthew 6:33: *"But seek first the kingdom of God and His righteousness, and all these things shall be added to you"* (NKJV). Message? "You aren't seeking hard enough! You have to seek better or you'll never measure up enough to get 'all these things.'"

It is really amazing how we can construct a believe system of our own, based on a combination of faulty theology, misapplied Scripture, and our own human frailty.

Not to mention expectations. We assume Scripture made certain promises that simply aren't there.

When you want something so badly that you invent a religious rationale, you set yourself up for disappointment. When your desire doesn't come through, God gets the blame. Meanwhile you experience disillusionment and possibly depression. And if you don't address your disappointment with God in a biblically accurate and emotionally healthy way, the depression can become debilitating.

ENTER ELIJAH

Elijah was as human as we are, and yet when he prayed earnestly that no rain would fall, none fell for three and a half years! Then, when he prayed again, the sky sent down rain and the earth began to yield its crops" (James 5:17–18 NLT).

Not only did he end the drought, Elijah was quite the prayer warrior. Wyatt Earp had his showdown at the OK Corral; William Wallace, his victory at Bannockburn — but Elijah fought a battle for the ages on the side of Almighty God!

Here's how it went down: Israel was far from God. They were following wicked King Ahab and his queen, Jezebel. They worshipped the false gods Asherah and Baal. God called on Elijah to confront his nation's apostasy, and he issued this challenge:

> *(King) Ahab went to meet Elijah. When he saw Elijah, he said to him, "Is that you, you troubler of Israel?"*
> *"I have not made trouble for Israel," Elijah replied. "But you and your father's family have. You have abandoned the Lord's commands and have followed the Baals. Now summon the people from all over Israel to meet me on Mount Carmel. And bring the four hundred and fifty prophets of Baal and the four hundred prophets of Asherah, who eat at Jezebel's table" (1 Kings 18:16–19).*

You can see what's happening. Elijah is getting ready to confront 450 false prophets with 400 hostile witnesses. Talk about outnumbered! The narrative continues:

> *So Ahab sent word throughout all Israel and assembled the prophets on Mount Carmel. Elijah went before the people and said, "How long will you waver between two opinions? If the Lord is God, follow him; but if Baal is God, follow him."*
> *But the people said nothing.*
> *Then Elijah said to them, "I am the only one of the Lord's prophets left, but Baal has four hundred and fifty prophets. Get two bulls for us. Let Baal's prophets choose one for themselves, and let them cut it into pieces and put it on the wood but not set fire to it. I will prepare the other bull and put it on the wood but not set fire to it. Then you call on the name of your god, and I will call on the name of the Lord. The god who answers by fire – he is God."*
> *Then all the people said, "What you say is good."*
> *Elijah said to the prophets of Baal, "Choose one of the bulls and prepare it first, since there are so many of you.*

Call on the name of your god, but do not light the fire." So they took the bull given them and prepared it.

Then they called on the name of Baal from morning till noon. "Baal, answer us!" they shouted. But there was no response; no one answered. And they danced around the altar they had made (vs. 20–26).

At this point, Elijah gets ornery, as we say in Indiana. He pours on the sarcasm.

At noon Elijah began to taunt them. "Shout louder!" he said. "Surely he is a god! Perhaps he is deep in thought, or busy, or traveling. Maybe he is sleeping and must be awakened." So they shouted louder and slashed themselves with swords and spears, as was their custom, until their blood flowed. Midday passed, and they continued their frantic prophesying until the time for the evening sacrifice. But there was no response, no one answered, no one paid attention (vs. 27–29).

At least four to seven hours of these idolatrous shenanigans went on. Then Elijah essentially said, "OK, guys, you've had your time. It's God's turn at bat."

Then Elijah said to all the people, "Come here to me." They came to him, and he repaired the altar of the Lord, which had been torn down. Elijah took twelve stones, one for each of the tribes descended from Jacob, to whom the word of the Lord had come, saying, "Your name shall be Israel." With the stones he built an altar in the name of the Lord, and he dug a trench around it large enough to hold two seahs of seed. He arranged the wood, cut the bull into pieces and laid it on the wood.

Then he said to them, "Fill four large jars with water and pour it on the offering and on the wood." "Do it again," he said, and they did it again. "Do it a third time," he ordered, and they did it the third time. The water ran down around the altar and even filled the trench (vs. 30–35).

Talk about stacking the deck! Why so much water, especially in a time of drought? Elijah anticipated the doubters and wanted to make it clear that this would not be "spontaneous combustion." It was a perfect setup.

At the time of sacrifice, the prophet Elijah stepped forward and prayed: "Lord, the God of Abraham, Isaac and Israel, let it be known today that you are God in Israel and that I am your servant and have done all these things at your command. Answer me, Lord, answer me, so these people will know that you, Lord, are God, and that you are turning their hearts back again."

Then the fire of the Lord fell and burned up the sacrifice, the wood, the stones and the soil, and also licked up the water in the trench. When all the people saw this, they fell prostrate and cried, "The Lord – he is God! The Lord – he is God!"

Then Elijah commanded them, "Seize the prophets of Baal. Don't let anyone get away!" They seized them, and Elijah had them brought down to the Kishon Valley and slaughtered there (vs. 36–40).

This is like a Hollywood script! The people shout affirmatively that Jehovah is the true God. They have a radical cleansing of false prophets from the land, and it appears the nation will repent and return to God.

At least that's what Elijah *expected*. However…

Now Ahab told Jezebel everything Elijah had done and how he had killed all the prophets with the sword. So Jezebel sent a messenger to Elijah to say, "May the gods deal with me, be it ever so severely, if by this time tomorrow I do not make your life like that of one of them.

Elijah was afraid and ran for his life (1 Kings 19:1–3).

What? He confronts the king of Israel, prays down fire from heaven, and takes down 450 hostile false prophets. Then a threat from a single person (albeit the queen of the land) sends him fleeing for his life?

What in the world happened?

To understand some of what's going on in the head of Elijah, we need to read on.

> *When he came to Beersheba in Judah, he left his servant there, while he himself went a day's journey into the wilderness. He came to a broom bush, sat down under it and prayed that he might die. "I have had enough, Lord," he said. "Take my life; I am no better than my ancestors." Then he lay down under the bush and fell asleep (1 Kings 19:3-5).*

Elijah was spiritually, physically, mentally, and emotionally exhausted. Spent. Fried. Worn to a frazzle. And why not?

- He had spent three years in hiding after declaring that it would not rain for three years (1 Kings 17, 18:10).
- He confronted the very people with the power and means to torture and kill him (18:15-19).
- He faced down 850 false prophets and had 450 of them executed (18:19, 40).
- He gave in to fear, ran for days over 150 miles from Carmel and Jezreel (northern Israel) to Be'er-Sheba (southern Israel) and on into the Negev wilderness.

All in a day's work, right?!

With all of that happening, miracle after miracle, you would think God would soon radically change hearts throughout the nation. But all Elijah got was a death threat from a still-wicked queen who had expanded Baal worship in Israel. No national (top-down) repentance. No acknowledgement from King Ahab that Jehovah really was God—even though Ahab had witnessed the entire event.

Disappointment leads to disillusionment—which, left unchecked, turns to depression.

My friend Ken Mahan, a youth pastor, once took a team of teens to minister at a county fair. They used martial arts, gymnastics, music, and drama to attract crowds. Then they would deliver the gospel.

The weather wouldn't cooperate. The team had traveled several hundred miles, this was their one day to perform. What did they do? They prayed for God to hold off the rain until after their presentation.

But God didn't answer that prayer. The kids' faith did not strengthen; it wavered. The youth director questioned God. Thanks to good theology, they eventually gave the whole thing to God. The rain was simply part of the mystery and wisdom of His sovereignty.

How did God address Elijah's depression episode? Read on.

All at once an angel touched him and said, "Get up and eat." He looked around, and there by his head was some bread baked over hot coals, and a jar of water. He ate and drank and then lay down again.

The angel of the Lord came back a second time and touched him and said, "Get up and eat, for the journey is too much for you." So he got up and ate and drank. Strengthened by that food, he traveled forty days and forty nights until he reached Horeb, the mountain of God. There he went into a cave and spent the night.

And the word of the Lord came to him: "What are you doing here, Elijah?"

He replied, "I have been very zealous for the Lord God Almighty. The Israelites have rejected your covenant, torn down your altars, and put your prophets to death with the sword. I am the only one left, and now they are trying to kill me too."

The Lord said, "Go out and stand on the mountain in the presence of the Lord, for the Lord is about to pass by."

Then a great and powerful wind tore the mountains apart and shattered the rocks before the Lord, but the Lord was not in the wind. After the wind there was an earthquake, but the Lord was not in the earthquake. After the earthquake came a fire, but the Lord was not in the fire.

41

And after the fire came a gentle whisper. When Elijah heard it, he pulled his cloak over his face and went out and stood at the mouth of the cave.

Then a voice said to him, "What are you doing here, Elijah?"

He replied, "I have been very zealous for the Lord God Almighty. The Israelites have rejected your covenant, torn down your altars, and put your prophets to death with the sword. I am the only one left, and now they are trying to kill me too."

The Lord said to him, "Go back the way you came...(and know that) I reserve seven thousand in Israel — all whose knees have not bowed down to Baal and whose mouths have not kissed him" (1 Kings 19:5–18).

Summary:

- God ministered to Elijah's physical needs (food and sleep).
- God took him on a forty-day journey to be alone and process the whole experience. Call it an extended debriefing time, if you will. When you're alone — really alone — with God, much becomes clear.
- After God demonstrated Himself to the nation in a bombastic way (fire from heaven), God spoke to Elijah in a *"still, small voice"* (19:12, KJV). So God does not always communicate through wind, earthquake, and fire.
- He allowed Elijah to vent not once but twice, recounting all that had happened and everything God had done and not done. He did it respectfully and honestly, and God heard him out.
- God then gave Elijah a new assignment: "Go back the way you came." This provided purpose, a reason to go on.
- God corrected a misconception. ("Elijah, you're not the only one. I still have seven thousand who are faithful to Me.")

After my 1991 recording contract debacle, I spent three years in the shadowlands of depression. God used the time to teach me a number of things about Him, His ways, and my expectations.

1. When you "sign up" to follow God, you give Him a blank sheet of paper with your signature at the bottom. He lovingly and purposefully fills in the details along the way. This includes unknown pains, losses, trials, and blessings.
2. Always remember Romans 8:28: *"And we know that in all things God works for the good of those who love Him, who have been called according to His purpose."* It really is true for everyone who calls on the name of Christ. It dovetails perfectly with Philippians 2:13: *"For it is God who works in you to will and to act according to His good purpose."* and Ephesians 2:10: *"For we are God's workmanship, created in Christ Jesus to do good works, which God prepared in advance for us to do."*
3. Another key passage is Paul's narrative in 2 Corinthians 12:7–10. Verse 9 is Jesus speaking: *"My grace is sufficient for you."*

That passage refers to a "thorn in the flesh" that Paul has to endure. Paul calls it a *"messenger of Satan"* (v. 7). Because Paul is doing God's work, the enemy afflicts him.

Just like Paul, I had to enter a season of spiritual warfare. But I knew almost nothing about it.

CHAPTER 5

BREAKING DOWN STRONGHOLDS

Repression: A mental process by which distressing thoughts, memories or impulses that may give rise to anxiety are excluded from consciousness and left to operate in the unconscious.[14]

The subject of repression is controversial. Many therapists and researchers conclude that repression of memories is possible in cases of trauma. To date, however, they see little scientific and empirical data to validate the diagnostic term known as "dissociative amnesia."[15] [16]

That said, most of us try subconsciously to move on from painful memories. We all do our share of stuffing and escaping. We use addictions, some acceptable and others less so, to distract ourselves from the pain of the memory.

The unacceptable addictions are obvious — drugs, alcohol, sexual perversion, and so on. The "acceptable" ones (but dysfunctional nevertheless) include things like career, volunteerism, and serving the Lord through the church. These are all good things, especially the last. We are called to serve Him and it can be rewarding and exhilarating. But if you do it for applause, kudos, or a form of escape, you might simply be running from the pain of your past.

You also become skilled over time at what I call mental gymnastics, especially in the Christian world. You construct narratives that rationalize your behavior so you can avoid responsibility from sins — whether of commission (what you shouldn't do) or omission (what you should do). You can recite all the "right" reasons for your actions when in reality your motives are selfish.

If you are a Christian, pause here and ask yourself:

- Why am I serving the Lord?
- Why am I doing (blank)?
- Why am I not doing (blank)?
- Why am I avoiding (blank)?

Take a moment to contemplate these questions and journal your response(s). Note that last blank may include specific people as well as things.

FOOTHOLDS AND STRONGHOLDS

Let's examine how sinful acts, whether coping methods or direct disobedience, develop from a foothold to a stronghold.

Ephesians 4:27 says, "Do not give the devil a foothold." The context demonstrates how the devil brings about a foothold in our lives.

Therefore each of you must put off falsehood and speak truthfully to your neighbor, for we are all members of one body. "In your anger do not sin": Do not let the sun go down while you are still angry, and do not give the devil a foothold (4:25–27).

Paul charges us to:

- "Be made *new* in the attitude of your minds," (v. 23, emphasis mine) and then to
- "Put on the *new* self, created to be like God in true righteousness and holiness," (v. 24, emphasis mine).

Paul then says:

- Put off falsehood (quit lying).
- Speak truthfully with your neighbor.
- In your anger do not sin (Note he doesn't say, "Don't be angry." Just don't sin when you are angry).
- Don't go to bed until you address the cause of your

anger and work things out between yourself and the person with whom you are angry.

When we live with this kind of focus on self-control by the power of the Holy Spirit, we gain the spiritual ability to obey verse 27 and not give the devil a foothold. We can keep the door shut. Otherwise we are at the mercy of the enemy.

It's kind of like the old door-to-door salesman who would stick his foot in the door while hawking his product so the resident couldn't shut him out.

Unchecked anger opens the door so the devil can stick his foot in and start talking. If you don't put on your new self in Christ, you can't slam the door. So you listen, subtly, to the devil's tempting sales pitch and make a purchase of indulgence.

If you keep doing this, the foothold eventually becomes a stronghold. By habit or rationalization, you believe your newly imposed reality. *This is just how I am. This is just how life is.*

> For though we live in the world, we do not wage war as the world does. The weapons we fight with are not the weapons of the world. On the contrary, they have divine power to demolish strongholds. We demolish arguments and every pretension that sets itself up against the knowledge of God, and we take captive every thought to make it obedient to Christ. And we will be ready to punish every act of disobedience, once your obedience is complete (2 Corinthians 10:3–6).

We will later identify the "weapons we fight with," but the point here is that strongholds are just that: strong holds. The Greek word is *ochuroma* (pronounced okh-oo'-ro-mah), which means "a heavily fortified containment." Paul uses it figuratively as a false argument in which a person "seeks shelter" ("a safe place") to escape reality.[17]

Also, "The word is not common in Classical Greek, but occurs frequently in the Apocrypha (non-canonical books from between the Old and New Testaments). In its use here there may lie a reminiscence of the rock-forts on the coast of Paul's native Cilicia, which were pulled down by the Romans in their attacks on the Cilician pirates."[18]

I am indebted to evangelist Rick Renner, missionary to the former Soviet Union, for his insights on strongholds. Here he describes two types of strongholds:

If you want to be free from every stronghold of the enemy in your life, you have to understand that there are two kinds of strongholds: rational and irrational. The rational strongholds are the more difficult to deal with — because they usually make sense!

Paul refers to these rational strongholds when he says, "Casting down imaginations…" The word imaginations is taken from the Greek word logismos, which is where we get the word logic," as in "logical thinking." Thank God for a good, sound mind, but even a sound mind must be submitted to the sanctifying work of the Holy Spirit. Otherwise, your mind will develop a stronghold of natural reasoning that starts to dictate all kinds of lies to your life. I call these rational strongholds.

…Your logical mind will always try to talk you out of obeying God. In fact, if you don't take charge of your mind, it will begin to completely dominate and control your (lack of) obedience to God. It will tell you that you can't afford to obey the Lord and that it isn't a good time to step out in faith. Your natural mind will come up with a whole host of logical reasons to explain why you shouldn't do what the Spirit of God is telling you to do.

Second, there are irrational strongholds. These primarily have to do with completely unrealistic fears and worries, such as a fear of contracting a terminal disease, a fear of dying early in life, an abnormal fear of rejection, and so forth. These types of irrational strongholds in the mind, emotions, and imagination will normally play their course and then dissipate. But if harassing thoughts persist in your mind and insist on controlling you mentally and emotionally, you must deal with them straightforwardly with the Word of God.

In Second Corinthians 10:5, Paul says, "Casting down imaginations, and every high thing that exalteth itself against the knowledge of God, and bringing into captivity every thought to the obedience of Christ," (KJV). Notice that Paul doesn't say one thing about bringing the devil into captivity. Rather, he tells you to take every thought into captivity to the obedience of Christ.

The devil tries to invade your life through lies that he plants in your brain. If you don't take your thoughts captive, it will be just a matter of time before the devil starts using those lies to create mental and emotional strongholds for the purpose of keeping you in bondage. But if you take your thoughts captive, then your thoughts cannot take you captive![19]

To Renner's categories of rational and irrational strongholds, I would like to add a third:

FORGOTTEN STRONGHOLDS

You'll recall in Chapter Two when I described how Jill, my counselor, took me back in time, asking the Holy Spirit to reveal anyone I needed to forgive or to ask forgiveness from. She called this my "History Work."

As we continued, I remembered another defining event...

I was fifteen. I had made an all-star team and was at least the second best pitcher on the team. I was also the better first baseman and had just under a .400 batting average for the season. So what happened?

The father of the other first baseman, "Jimmy Green," came out to help with the travel and organizing of the all-star team. "Mr. Green" became the guy parents sought with questions or issues so the coach could focus on coaching.

Now, Jimmy was also good. After all, he was on the all-star team too. But I was…well…better. I had the better batting and fielding averages. Nevertheless, the coach came to me and my dad (one of two assistant coaches) and said I should be ready to pitch because Jimmy would be on first base.

I sucked it up. This was my first acquaintance with politics.

Game one, Coach selected one of the pitchers from the team he coached during the season — one of "his" players — to start. Close game, we won. I rode the bench.

Game two, Coach selected a pitcher that was a bit of a surprise. We needed relief pitching, and he didn't pick me. We won another close game. I rode the bench.

It was a double-elimination tournament, so I got to pitch the third game. If I lost, we'd have another opportunity to win. My game was the one we could "afford to lose."

I didn't tell the coach I had a blister on my left middle finger where I gripped my curveball. That meant I had only one pitch — my fastball. So I threw mostly fastballs and changeups. I threw a two-hit shutout, and we won 10-0. We were off to the next leg of the tournament the following weekend.

I thought, "OK, another week to heal up the finger, I'll probably get the first start."

I didn't. I rode the bench and we lost game #1. One more loss and we were out of the tournament.

The next game we were down 7–5 in the top of the last inning. They were up to bat with a runner on base, nobody out. That was when I heard my name. "Kaufman, get ready!"

I warmed up quickly. By the time I got the ball, bases were loaded, one out. And was I angry. So angry that my first pitch was wild. I raced to the plate as the runner from third was coming in to score. The catcher threw me the ball just as the runner arrived. I stiffened for the hit, tagged him, and held onto the ball. He was *out!*

I then proceeded to strike out the batter on the nex'
pitches. Three outs, and we were coming up for our last at-υ..

As I walked off the mound to the dugout, I stared at
Coach. He refused to look at me. Guilt will do that.

Oh, by the way...we lost 7–5 with two runners on base. I
was in the on-deck circle when the guy ahead of me made the
last out of the game. I like to think I would have made a
difference if I'd had the chance to bat.

The anger ("be angry and sin not") was unchecked. That
was the seed of bitterness, freshly planted.

All that to say...I wish it didn't affect me the way it did. I
wish I had been more mature and handled it differently. I
wish I'd had a godly mentor to say "Tim, what happened,
happened. But your loving Heavenly Father allowed it for a
deeper purpose. I want to pray for you right now and
challenge you to forgive the wrong this authority figure did
in your life. There's something bigger going on here." Then,
perhaps, I would've handled it differently and avoided the
foothold and eventual stronghold of bitterness.

But I didn't. At age fifteen, I didn't know how to process
acceptance of situations and forgiveness of offenders. This
was too big a deal. At least to me it was. So I stuffed my anger
and bitterness toward that coach. I carried it into my vocation,
my marriage, and my other relationships. It stayed with me
for twenty-two years!

Twenty...two...years...

This incident reinforced the recording: "not (quite) good
enough." Then a voice would continue to say, for weeks and
months afterward, "Yeah, you were good enough to *make* the
all-star team, but good enough to start? Never! If only you
were better—so good that they couldn't ignore you—*then*
you'd be good enough."

Once I forgave this coach in Jill's counseling office, I began
to be free of this defining event.

A STRONGHOLD BROKEN!

As we continued with my history work, through prayer, I entered a vision. I saw myself in my bedroom at age eight or nine. I had had a bad dream.

Usually in this situation, Mom and Dad would come over to the bed, Mom would sit on the edge, and both would comfort me. She would rub my arms or head, and their words of encouragement would get me back to sleep.

But this time, they stood at the door, comforting me from afar. They were saying all the right things, but the distance was confusing.

But then Jesus came into the room, moved past them, and knelt by my bed. He touched my upper left arm with a comforting smile. "Tim, it's okay, I'm here."

I sat up on my right elbow. "Can I trust You? Can I *really* trust You?"

Then He looked me right in the eyes. "Tim, I will be with you, and I will be in you" (what He told us all in John 14:17). When He uttered the last two words, "in you," his body merged with mine. He literally came into me.

I began to weep with a joy I'd never known. After some time, I shared the vision with Jill. She confirmed that it was a significant breakthrough.

Interestingly, on the two-and-a-half-hour drive home, I suddenly realized something: For the first time, I could pray to Jesus on a first-name basis. No longer was He just "The Lord"; He was truly my brother (Hebrews 2:11–12). I still relate to Jesus as Lord, Teacher, Master, and other names. But just as comfortable, or even more so, is the name *Jesus*.

I realize what I've just shared will probably close some doors of ministry in certain circles and open some doors in others. That's okay. I contend that God meets us where we are, not where we should be. And He'll use any means necessary to reach us in our brokenness. Heck, some think that it's the spiritual people who have such experiences. But you can also look at it this way: maybe those of us who have had such experiences needed them because we're not all that spiritual! Our exposed deep need required something radical to reach us. It's something to think about.

CONFUSION

One would think that after such an incredible breakthrough, the depression would be over, replaced by perpetual joy.

My depression continued, however, much to my dismay and that of my family. I was praying differently and seeing the Scriptures with new eyes, but the dogged emotional cloud of despair would still emerge anytime and yank me down again. With the advantage of hindsight, I'm convince this is where medication would have made a difference.

But I also gained some insight into a Bible story that had always been a major puzzle.

TAKE TWO

When they arrived at Bethsaida, some people brought a blind man to Jesus, and they begged him to touch the man and heal him. Jesus took the blind man by the hand and led him out of the village. Then, spitting on the man's eyes, he laid his hands on him and asked, "Can you see anything now?" The man looked around. "Yes," he said, "I see people," **but I can't see them very clearly.** *They look like trees walking around." Then Jesus placed his hands on the man's eyes* **again,** *and his eyes were opened. His sight was* **completely restored,** *and* **he could see everything clearly** (Mark 8:22–25 NLT, emphasis mine).

Huh? While Jesus was healing the man the first time, was there a short circuit? He could only see blurry people.

Did the man not have enough faith? Why did Jesus take two stages to heal this man? It's the only time anything like this occurs in the miracles of Jesus.

Alexander MacLaren gives this interesting insight as to why Jesus did a "take two," as it were:

> *Now I take it that the worthiest view of that strangely protracted process, broken up into two halves by the question that is dropped into the middle, is this...that it was determined by the man's faith, and was meant to increase it. He was healed slowly because he believed slowly. His faith was a condition of his cure, and the measure of it determined the measure of the restoration; and the rate of the growth of his faith settled the rate of the perfecting of Christ's work on him. As a rule, faith in His power to heal was a condition of Christ's healing, and that mainly because our Lord would rather make men believing than sound of body. They often wanted only the outward miracle, but He wanted to make it the means of insinuating a better healing into their spirits. And so, not that there was any necessary connection between their faith and the exercise of His miraculous power, but in order that He might bless them with His best gifts, He usually worked on the principle "According to your faith be it unto you." And here, as a nurse or a mother with her child might do, He keeps step with the little steps, and goes slowly because the man goes slowly.[20]*

As I look back, I believe that if I had healed completely and immediately, I would have had something of a spiritual short circuit. Jesus acts lovingly, compassionately, wisely, and perfectly. He has His reasons, and we can trust He's doing what's best for us and His glory.

As I limped through from 1992 to 1994, I have to confess I found the extremely slow pace of recovery discouraging. But one morning in August of 1994, I sat at my office desk reading from my Bible, and suddenly, the cloud again lifted. I was at peace again. I didn't understand how or why it happened *that* day, but I was just glad.

Interestingly, that morning I penned a few seed thoughts that would eventually become "His Mercies Are New to Me," the title song on a future CD.

Ah, how God works.

CHAPTER 6

HE WILL PROVIDE

When hope seems far from where you are
And your blue skies all have turned gray
Your path's unclear and failures' fears
Are standing in your way
Hold tightly to God's promise
Every need He will supply
For though the world may fall around us
On this we can rely: He will provide [21]

The spring of 1995 was a seminal time in our ministry. After I knew I would still sing and teach itinerantly, we basically had a relaunch in earnest. But this time, Alicia would be my "agent." She would schedule the calendar; I would develop music and materials. We put our shoulders to the plow, knowing we were following the clear leading of the Lord. For three years, I made over 120 ministry appearances a year and began the writing for and production of album #10.

Then we almost lost Alicia in the birth of our fifth child, Naomi, on January 20, 1998.

After twenty-nine hours of labor, Alicia had two internal organs rupture and lost half of her blood. She was in ICU and Critical Care for a week. She was in bed at home for three months, taking a year and ten months to fully recover. Those first three months were a test for us as a family in many ways, but during this season, a song I'd long struggled to write came to me in one night. The song, fleshed out by my gifted cowriter, is "Let It Hurt." I would sing it for almost a decade, but I'd have to live it even more than I ever had before.

My "Not good enough, never have enough" mental tape would still play sometimes, though at a lower volume. You know, like the song you can't get out of your head?

In 2002, I was approaching age forty-nine with basically nothing for our retirement. How could we make up for lost time? Real estate seemed the best logical answer. We had several friends successful in real estate; it was a strong area of interest for Alicia, and we took some courses. Our first investment garnered us almost $7,000 in a quick flip of only two weeks. Our next venture involved a rehab. We had to hold it for eight months, but we still made $16,000. We then leveraged that into two rental homes, and we were off! The goal was to have several houses that would be income-producing properties for our retirement.

But we all know what happened in 2008–09.

DON'T TRY THIS AT HOME!

I had been on antidepressants since the spring of 2003, and they worked pretty well up until the winter of 2009. A well-meaning friend, also struggling with depression, shared how he had recently gone off of his meds with great success. He then made the case that my drugs had this or that side effect, and he had some impressive references and documentation (but zero data—so don't try this on your own!)

So...I tried to go off—cold turkey, without consulting my doctor. Very stupid. I was a mess for two weeks. I immediately went back on, settled, and then tried to wean myself off.

Success—or so I thought.

Stay with me here. This is relevant.

From 2004 to January of 2010, I served as interim worship leader for Northcliffe Church, which required a two-hour commute. I would travel twice a week to lead a congregation of 1,000-plus parishioners in music ministry. I loved it. As co-laborers in the Lord's vineyard, the pastor and I became good friends. Strangely, I never felt inner peace to take the position full time, even though that would have make sense. I honestly tried three times to go in that direction, but the Holy Spirit urged me to stay put. And for good reasons.

The third time, in February 2009, the Lord said to my heart, "Tim, I know what you are trying to do. You want to anchor your finances with a steady income. You want to serve in a place you like, a place that likes you. All of this makes natural sense. But you are not to go. If you try to go through this open door again, it will be disobedience."

It could not have been clearer to me if it had been audible. If you track well with the Lord, you know what I'm talking about. It's a parallel to what the Apostle Paul experienced in II Corinthians 2:12-13:

> *When I came to Troas to preach the gospel of Christ, even though a door was opened for me in the Lord, my spirit was not at rest...so I...went on to Macedonia.* (ESV).

I will try to condense the rest of 2009 as the setup year for my January 2010 crash.

Two miraculous answers to prayer in the summer of 2009 led to me re-record a patriotic song I'd done in 1976, "I Believe in America." Given where our country was politically, I felt quite sure that "I Believe in America" could possibly become the next "God Bless America" or "God Bless the U.S.A." I would record it on an album with another patriotic song I wrote.

I raised money and hired an arranger. We produced the song with the finest players in Nashville and released it in the early fall of 2009—and it was a dud.

The song wasn't the problem. It was the arrangement. And basically, I was the arranger. Oh, my official arranger put the parts on the manuscript, but he did what I had told him to do.

And it flopped.

Now the tape was up full volume: NOT GOOD ENOUGH!

Meanwhile, "Fellowship Church," a large church close to my home, considered hiring me. We started initial talks that seemed promising. But with the economy struggling, Fellowship Church had three position needs but only enough resources for two. They passed over me. Again…NOT GOOD ENOUGH!

Not only did our real estate business suffer to the point of liquidation, but a home-based business we started in 2006 that had earned half our income the previous year became another victim of the economy.

Again…NEVER HAVE ENOUGH!

And finally, to my surprise, Northcliffe hired a full-time music director. My last month would be January 2010.

Because of the economy, music style, and worship format changes, churches were not scheduling concert artists as they once had.

The deck was stacked! Vocationally, I had nothing to go to or fall back on.

And my self-talk message was:

Even if something did open up, why try? You are NOT GOOD ENOUGH! Something would go wrong with it, just like it has with

- real estate.
- your church job.
- your music projects.
- your bookings and concerts.

No one wants what you have to sing, say, or sell anymore.

I was in bad shape from Thanksgiving 2009 until that January morning when I could no longer hold back the emotional tonnage.

I felt God had set me up. I'd heard from Him. I'd obeyed Him. I had done what He'd asked of me.

And it wasn't good enough. So I would never have enough.

There's a popular song that says, "When the darkness closes in, Lord, still I will say, 'Blessed be the Name of the Lord.'"

I couldn't. And I wouldn't.

It was all a setup. I'd never be good enough, so why try anymore?

In my bitterness toward God, I began to play the comparison game. I would think of other gospel music professionals and then ask Him, "You gave him/her a successful career and recording contract. They have a booking agent. They have a full calendar, even in this down time. And I'm just as good, talent-wise, but I must not be as good a person, as good a minister, as good as I need to be to have that blessing upon me."

Then I would be angry that He didn't make me like him/her…good enough as a person. After all, isn't He the one who "works in you, both to will and to do His good pleasure"?[22] And isn't He the one who "makes men holy"?[23]

I began to question everything I thought I knew about the kindness and provision of God as a good Father. I could not trust Him. Somehow this journey of faith had brought me to this place professionally and financially. Now that I was a failure as a family provider, the self-talk monologue went something like this:

> *God…You haven't come through. You could have made me good enough. Then I'd be emotionally healthy and therefore good enough to pursue whatever I was to pursue successfully. After all, God, doesn't Your word say, "It is the Lord who gives you the power to get wealth?" God, I'm not looking for a million dollars here. I'm a professional and good at what I do! After all these years, at my age, all I'm looking for is a stable income. You could do this. You've done it for so many of my peers, and you've left me out! But if I try…I'm supposed to try, right? I'm supposed to be responsible and take up what I am skilled and trained at, right? But I only end up where I started — not good enough!!!!! GOD…WHERE ARE YOU?!!!*

I felt like hell. I could no longer live like this. In fact, I really no longer wanted to live. I was done, finished. If this was all I could expect in life—a constant cycle of small wins followed by big failures—no more. NO MORE! Do you hear me? Is anyone listening?

It was like the saying, "Three steps forward, two steps back." Except those last seven years, leading up to January 8, 2010, were more like one step forward, and three steps back. I was swimming against a riptide. You struggle, and then fear takes hold. You work harder, you become desperate, and tire yourself out. Finally, you have no strength left.

Under I went.

I had fully bought into the lie that God was not good.

TIME OUT!

A unique phenomenon happens in almost every competitive basketball game between two good teams. They will play close, so the score is almost never more than three or four points apart. Then, all of a sudden, one of the teams goes on a "run."

They make a three-point shot, steal the ball, make another three-pointer, and keep the other team from scoring several trips down the floor. All the while, they make every shot when they have the ball. A once competitive game becomes one team with a twelve-point lead, just like that!

And the coach jumps up and calls, "Time out!"

Often a run will happen just before halftime. And man, is the non-running team glad to see the game clock stop! Finally they can go into the locker room and:

- Rehydrate.
- Refresh.
- Rest.
- Regroup mentally.
- Re-strategize with the coach.
- Refocus.
- Reenter the game with Renewed hope!

Sometimes life makes a "run" at us. And we have aside and:

- Refresh ourselves mentally, emotionally, physically, spiritually.
- Remember how God has worked in the past.
- Reformulate strategies in new ways (with others' input so we don't make the same mistakes again).
- Refocus on the main purpose of our life.
- Reengage.

Notice how I've reused the prefix *re* repeatedly here. Why is that? Simple. It's because *once* upon a time, we were fresh with ideas, plans, and aspirations. *Once* we formulated a life strategy (career path, family goals, and such). *Once* we were focused; we knew what we wanted and why. *Once* we engaged in that main purpose of our life.

Then we got sidetracked. Jesus calls it, "the cares (worries) of this life" (see Mark 4:1–20). He states that the worries of this life are:

1. The deceitfulness of wealth, and
2. The desires for other things

These distractions "choke the Word, making it unfruitful" (v. 19). In other words, we become preoccupied with other things.

As your "coach," may I call a time out for you right now? Let me ask you some questions.

- What were you once envisioning your life to be or look like?
- What were you born and built to do?
- What did you once aspire to, dream about, fully engage in?
- What gives, or maybe, gave you life?

A few more questions:

- What (or who) distracted you or took your eye off the ball?
- What (or who) detoured you or took you off course, the path you were on?
- What (or who) became the new object of your affection or commitment?
- Where are you right now?

Part of what happened to me is that I got distracted, big time. I thought I had to become my provider. I thought I had to come up with a solution rather than live out my "Levitical calling."[24] I needed to trust God to be our perpetual "Jehovah Jireh" (The Lord Who Provides).

During this season, I read several scriptures that offered me both confrontation and comfort with timely and appropriate words. For example:

> Who among you fears the Lord and obeys his Servant? If such men walk in darkness, without one ray of light, let them trust the Lord, let them rely upon their God. But see here, you who live in **your own light** and warm yourselves from **your own fires** and not from God's; you will live among sorrows (Isaiah 50:10–11 TLB, emphasis mine).

Many times, we make decisions that seem rational and measured but often just appear that way. For example, we genuinely needed extra income. I could have gotten a regular hourly or contract job. Instead I decided to start a home-based business — much more responsibility. I think this distraction contributed to me losing ministry focus and eventually confusing my calling. I lit my own fire to see where I was supposed to go. But God has already provided a light for our direction in life…

> Thy word is a lamp unto my feet, and a light unto my path (Psalms 119:105 KJV).

Distractions abound. But time and again I come back to this story to help me refocus on what is quintessentially important.

> *Now it happened as they went that He entered a certain village; and a certain woman named Martha welcomed Him into her house. And she had a sister called Mary, who also sat at Jesus' feet and heard His word. But Martha was distracted with much serving, and she approached Him and said, "Lord, do You not care that my sister has left me to serve alone? Therefore tell her to help me."*
>
> *And Jesus answered and said to her, "Martha, Martha, you are worried and troubled about **many things**. But **one thing** is needed, and Mary has chosen that good part, which will not be taken away from her" (Luke 10:38–42 NKJV, emphasis mine).*

Martha was distracted by the many things (plural), but Jesus says there's only one thing (singular) that we need in our life: to be at His feet in worship and learning.

But what about the preparations Martha had hanging over her head? What about the regular stuff of life that we all need to take care of—kids, schedules, career, chores, hobbies, etc.?

Those are very legitimate questions. How many of us feel that when we should be spending time with God, life just gets in the way?

Stay with me here. Look at these two other verses Jesus gives us as balanced instruction.

> *But seek first the kingdom of God and His righteousness, and all these **things (plural)** shall be added to you* (Matthew 6:33 NKJV, emphasis mine).

> *If you then, who are evil, know how to give good gifts to your children, how much more will your Father who is in heaven give good **things (plural)** to those who ask him!* (Matthew 7:11 ESV, emphasis mine).

Again...*But one* **thing (singular)** *is needed, and Mary has chosen that good part, which will not be taken away from her* (Luke 10:42, emphasis mine).

Jesus is saying to Martha—and to you and to me: "You take care of the one thing, fellowship with Me, and I'll take care of the things (plural) that you need in your life. Leave those things (plural) to Me."

Bottom line?

- "Seek first My kingdom" (Jesus' rule in your life).
- "Seek first My righteousness" (Jesus' standard of living in your life).
- "I'll take care of the rest" (Jesus' call to trust Him).

About two weeks after that awful Friday in January 2010, Alicia scheduled an appointment to get me up and out of the house. As I drove along, silent and barely even feeling anything, Alicia in the passenger seat answered a cell phone call.

The caller said, "Every year, we donate from our stock options, and we usually give it to our church. But last night as we prayed, we both sensed God telling us to give it to your ministry. So that we can get the proper paperwork, is your ministry a not-for-profit?"

Alicia said yes, and they got the process started.

The first week of March, we received over $7,000 deposited into our ministry account! It was a welcome provision since I'd just cashed my last severance check.

Things remained lean that year, but He provided three months' worth of food from the local food pantry. Those months also provided a heavy dose of humility.

God will provide. He will provide what we need most, whether it is financial, spiritual, emotional, life lessons—whatever—He will provide for His own.

And He will provide for you, my friend.

A smile may hide the tears inside
And your burden's so hard to bear
Sometimes it seems your plans and dreams
Have ended in despair
The wind and waves may threaten
And the storms of life may blow
But tho' all else may seem uncertain
This one thing we know

CHORUS
He will provide, He will provide
When times are hard and God seems far
He will provide
This season will not last forever
You'll hope again, this storm you'll weather
In time you'll see, much more than ever
He will provide [25]

CHAPTER 7
THE LONG ROAD BACK

"The only thing we have to fear, is fear itself."
—President Franklin D. Roosevelt, December 7, 1941

I started to write, "Have you ever been afraid of...?" but I thought better of it. The real question is "Of what have you ever been afraid?"

All of us have fears, right? Most of us battle several fears. Here are some common ones:

- Falling
- Water (drowning)
- Heights
- The dark
- Crowds
- Flying (Famed NFL Football coach John Madden was so afraid of it that he bought a tour bus to get from city to city.)
- Illness
- Public speaking (the biggest fear, statistically)
- Success
- Failure

When we've experienced failure after failure, whether perceived or true, we hold fast to our fears through discouragement or even the mere potential of it. We just don't want to go there again.

"Reverend Snow," a well-known Midwestern pastor recorded in an immoral phone conversation, had to resign from his church. Four pastors and a businessman helped Snow rebuild his life and start a financial consultancy. Several years later, his partner embezzled most of the firm's assets, and Snow took his life.

My pastor at the time, Rev. Herbert Fitzpatrick, was a friend of Snow. I asked him why Snow would resort to suicide.

Pastor Fitz replied, "I think he was just too embarrassed and afraid to try again."

Bingo.

For some, a comeback is truly difficult, but it's not impossible. Many people have made huge mistakes, struggled mightily, and conquered not only circumstances but their fears as well. And we begin with one small step.

SIGNS ALONG THE WAY

Today you may be clinically depressed, mildly depressed, or just somewhat disappointed. Whatever your state, if you take a small step, God will meet you where you are and help you with the subsequent steps. God will give you what I call "signs along the way" to encourage you to take the next step, small as it may be.

THE DITCH

"Dad, I wrecked the car."

Click.

I had to call him back again and repeat that I had wrecked the car. I found out later that he hung up because he thought he had dreamt it.

My mom shook him. "Who was that?"

Dad said, "I think it was Tim…something about a wreck."

"And you hung up on him?!"

I cut dad a break because it was after midnight. He cut me a break because it was, well, an accident.

My two sisters and I were coming home from a friend's house after watching the first World Series night game in history (for you sports history buffs, it was in 1971 between the Pittsburgh Pirates and the Baltimore Orioles). I was on an unfamiliar road in extreme fog. I was going a little too fast for the conditions, and suddenly we couldn't even see the front of the car. When I came out of the haze, a big, yellow sign with a big, black arrow pointing left loomed directly in front of me!

I hit the brakes, and my sisters screamed. We slid through the shallow ditch, split a barbed wired fence (sparks flew), and romped into a cornfield. The car came to rest, and my first thought was, "Dad is really gonna be ticked."

I needed to find a phone. (This was 1971, remember? No cell phones.) I walked a mile to a farmhouse, and woke the farmer. He was grouchy as expected, but his nice wife smoothed things over. I called home, and the sheriff was there in an hour with the tow truck driver (woke them up too). Two hours later the girls were in bed. Dad, Mom, and I "debriefed."

I'll never ever forget that big, yellow sign with the big, black arrow. It was like some high authority pointing "THIS WAY."

THE FOG

Sometimes in our process of overcoming depression, everything is a fog. We can't see very far ahead. But if we slow down and proceed deliberately and intentionally, we will see timely signs that will point us in the right direction. Then we don't end up in a cornfield...or a hospital...or a morgue.

We have to look for the "signs along the way" (SATW).

I want to make one thing clear regarding these signs. They are not curative in themselves. They are more sustentative. They help us to keep going, to keep putting one foot in front of the other in our journey toward wholeness and health. They say to us, "God is up to something after all. You don't have to give up just yet. You can keep going." In fact, often we want to keep going just to see what the next sign is!

Here's what happened, sequentially, in just the first few months of this long road back:

1. The first SATW provided the introduction for this book: Lorraine's providential arrival at our home, giving Alicia the clarity that my condition was serious and we needed to see a doctor immediately.

2. The second SATW was the next evening as Alicia and I decided to attend the Saturday night service at our home church, First Baptist of Orlando. Our associate pastor, Jimmy Knott, was the speaker. His son had committed suicide a few years earlier, and Jimmy and his family had gone through the deepest of waters. He spoke that night on courage. "Fear not" became a seed planted in my heart and mind. Just a seed, but something that would germinate over time. I can remember it like yesterday. His text was Joshua 1:9: *"Have I not commanded you? Be strong and courageous.* **Do not be frightened***, and do not be dismayed, for the Lord your God is with you wherever you go"* (ESV emphasis mine).

3. The next SATW was that surprise $7,000 gift to our ministry, just days later.

4. That same week, Alicia and I visited our church staff lead counselor, Dr. Charles Bell. He arranged for the church to subsidize my psychiatrist visits, and the doctor supplied my meds through his inventory of samples.

5. We also met our counselor, Bob. This skilled therapist helped greatly. He still does, and he's become a faithful friend. Our "sessions" now are visits to a local coffee shop.

6. I had one concert in March, one in April, and did not have another until July. From then through September, as I mentioned earlier, the local food pantry helped us get by. Plus, we had to drive two borrowed automobiles, one of them for two years.

Humbling? Yes. Was God teaching us many lessons? Yes. I still don't know how we covered rent, food, gas, and basic bills. But somehow, we did. God did. He took us through deep waters, but somehow each day he supplied our "daily bread," which was His daily "signs along the way."

Your ears shall hear a word behind you, saying, "This is the way, walk in it," Whenever you turn to the right hand or whenever you turn to the left (Isaiah 30:21, NKJV).

SELF-SABOTAGE

In July of 2010, Alicia asked if I was going to continue with the new home-based business I had started in April.

"Honey, you know how entrepreneurship works. You've got to have a healthy mental outlook to succeed big. I really think I need to just go work on me."

She said, "Good. I'll take over if you aren't involved!" She understood that I meant I had to go to work on "not good enough; never have enough." Otherwise, I would just repeat the same pattern I had always known—self-sabotage.

Our business grew under Alicia's tenacity and skill. But even if I wanted to help I just couldn't do it. In the fall of 2010, I finally found part-time work as an interim music director in a small church about two hours from home. That wasn't enough, so I obtained my life insurance license in the spring of 2011. That venture lasted all of three months. I sold four policies.

I wanted to sing again, but I was so ashamed when I did take the platform for an occasional concert, my self-doubt and double-mindedness were unceasingly overwhelming and debilitating. It was a *very* low time for me.

When is a depressed person most susceptible to suicide? Contrary to what you might think, it's not when they hit bottom. Bob (my counselor) explained that it's just as they are coming up from the bottom.

When you *begin* to have a slight, miniscule ray of hope again, your reasoning powers return. Then you think, "This is too hard. This is too involved. The long road back is *too* long, and I don't have the stamina for it. I could do all this hard work of getting mentally healthy, but there's no guarantee that anything will really change. I've tried so many times. Why should I think anything will be different this time? I've done it all. Counseling, books, journaling, accountability groups, yada, yada, yada. And I'm still here. Why the hell am I thinking that anything will get better?"

That's when you're ripe for suicide, and I was right there.

Things were going better for us financially as Alicia's business succeeded. We were making financial progress and she had earned a monthly car allowance.

Me? I was still in counseling, singing very little. I was up one day and down the next. Those emotional swings came from my faulty thinking and attitude.

Counselor Bob shared with me the three areas of mental health we needed to address. Per his best guesstimate, my breakdown was:

- Chemical—sixty percent (addressed by proper medication)
- Cognitive—thirty percent (the way I was thinking/not thinking)
- Physical—ten percent (diet, exercise)

He said, "Tim, I may be off five to ten percent in these, but I don't think any more than that. The psychiatrist has helped you with #1, chemical. My conversation with him gives me confidence that you are on the right amounts of the right medications. You are doing well, as you have for years, in category #3, diet and exercise.

"Where I can help and where you need the most help is in area #2, how you think. It's how you view life and what you tell yourself about yourself. It's how you interpret the past, including the lies you've come to believe about who you are as a person, husband, father, and minister. Tim, you're a good man."

Of course, my nagging question was still, am I "good enough?"

Joyce Meyer, in her book *Battlefield for the Mind*, shares that one of her biggest challenges in overcoming past abuse issues was that she had to "think about what she was thinking about."

> *My mind was a mess! I was thinking all the wrong things. I went to church, and had done so for years, but I never actually thought about what I heard. It went in one ear and out the other, so to speak. I read some Scriptures in the Bible every day, but never thought about what I was reading. I was not attending to the Word. I was not giving any thought and study to what I was hearing. Therefore, no (increase in understanding) was coming back to me.*[26]

When we don't think right the enemy has fertile ground in which to plant seeds of doubt and unbelief. We begin to think all sorts of erroneous thoughts about God and we doubt His goodness.

ANSWERED PRAYER?

Do you believe God answers prayer? If you're like me, you would probably respond, "Yes, of course He does." But under your breath, you would add, "...for others, but not for me."

That's what I believed. And even when God would answer my prayers for some need, I would view it (due to erroneous thinking) as His provision for Alicia or the kids. Or God just wanted to assert His presence and control. But He didn't do it because He loved *me* and wanted to be a Father to *me*. I just wasn't "good enough" to warrant that kind of favor.

This lie was so entrenched that in January of 2011, I screamed the following to Alicia (hurting my voice so I could hardly speak for two days):

"I HAVE DONE EVERYTHING I KNOW TO DO AND I'M STILL NO DIFFERENT! WHY DOES GOD HATE ME? WHY DOES HE HOLD OUT ON ME? I'VE PRAYED AND PRAYED AND BEGGED AND PLEADED FOR HIM TO MAKE ME EMOTIONALLY HEALTHY AND WHOLE, AND NOTHING IS HAPPENING! AND NOTHING EVER WILL HAPPEN!"

I staggered into our living room, fell to the floor, put my head in the chair, and heaved heavy sobs for what seemed like an hour.

I know this transparency will make a few of you uncomfortable. That's okay; you're in good company. Let's quit pretending we have it all together. Let's honestly face the hurts, habits, and hang-ups that are keeping us from the abundant life Jesus promised in John 10:10:

> *The thief (devil) does not come except to steal, and to kill, and to destroy. I (Jesus) have come that they may have life, and that they may have it more abundantly* (NKJV).

The biblical writers were gut-level honest. We need to be also.

- *For sighing has become my daily food; my groans pour out like water (Job 3:24).*

- *I am worn out from my groaning. All night long I flood my bed with weeping and drench my couch with tears (Psalms 6:6).*

- *My tears have been my food day and night, while people say to me all day long, "Where is your God?" (Psalms 42:3).*

- *How long, Lord God Almighty, will Your anger smolder against the prayers of Your people? You have fed them with the bread of tears; You have made them drink tears by the bowlful (Psalms 80:4–5).*

- *My groans are many and my heart is faint (Lamentations 1:22).*

The heaving slowed, the tears continued, and the battle for my mind began. I almost lost it again in July. Once again the lack of a gun in our house may have saved me. I don't know if I'd have used it. But I do understand now why people take their lives. When you feel overcome with the sense that nothing will ever change, death seems a welcome release.

Yet circumstances were changing, even if I wasn't. Alicia brought in enough income that I didn't have to work. That pressure was off, so I began to focus on getting well...really getting well.

2012 came and went. I began journaling and continued to meet with Bob. While I didn't sense any radical change, it was ever so slowly taking place.

SURPRISED BY A PLEASANT REJECTION

In early 2013, I began to think about writing this book. Immediately the old tapes started: "It won't be good enough, so why waste your time?" I shared my thoughts with Alicia.

"What difference does it make if anyone reads it? If it's the 'next thing' for you, just write it."

The wound of the ill-fated "I Believe in America" was still festering from 2009. Why should I waste time on writing when I should be working? But then, that was my work — wasn't it?

In April, I got one of those emails about e-book publishing. "Write and publish your e-book in a weekend," it promised. The seminar was free, so I attended — along with about 150 others. We worked on our respective books from Friday evening through Sunday.

I did finish the outline intro, and first chapter. In one of the workshops, a roundtable discussion suggested the title.

I came home, jazzed to write, and finished the book over the summer. I sent it to my daughter Amber, an English major, to proofread and suggest changes. I thought it would be up on Amazon by September.

Also getting ready for her wedding in October, Amber said I'd have to hold off until after Thanksgiving. Then: "Uh, Daddy, I didn't want to say this, but — we need to do a complete rewrite. Your book, as it is, has already been written ten times, and there's too much that needs to be said, but in a more real, raw, and transparent way. And remember, we went through it with you too. That's why I think we need to co-write it."

Rejection.

At first, the tape cued up to play: "See? Told ya it wasn't good enough!" But this time I managed to hit the OFF button and think differently. "Hey, this is good. She's right, it would be better with a weave of the family's perspective. Plus, every book goes through several drafts. Better yet, we can work together as father and daughter. Besides, it really wasn't good enough the first time. Which means it'll be better the second time — and third, and fourth if necessary, until we get it right. And maybe it is just for the journey of writing it together. If it helps us as a family, then so be it."

Progress. I wasn't afraid to begin trying again.

And neither should you. You have a story — a message that the world, your circle of influence, needs to hear. Face it. Live it. Tell it.

"Fear not."

CHAPTER 8

FACING SABOTAGE

*"We cannot solve our problems with the
same thinking we used to create them."*
– Albert Einstein[27]

I f you go to enough motivational thinking seminars, you will inevitably hear things like:

- "What your mind can conceive, you can achieve."
- "You gotta get rid of that 'stinkin' thinkin''!"
- "If you can see it in your mind's eye, you can have it by and by."
- "Once you replace negative thoughts with positive ones, you'll start having positive results."
- "Pessimism leads to weakness, optimism to power."

Yada, yada, yada…

Don't get me wrong. These quotes and others like them are true enough…for the most part. But if you suffer from depression, you've tried to "think differently" over and over again. As a Christian, you've memorized scripture, made positive truth confessions, and made massive efforts to help get your thinking straight, with little result.

Why?

Because all that activity is in the conscious mind. For the most part, your battle is against your sub-conscious mind – your core self. It's where you really believe what you believe about yourself. And no amount of positive self-talk will get you past it.

But it is part of the process.

Basic CBT (Cognitive Behavior Therapy) hypothesizes that *"people's thoughts and feelings are not determined by a situation, but by their interpretation and construction of the situation.* Recognizing this discrepancy, CBT seeks to modify the dysfunctional *core beliefs* that result in *automatic thoughts* which trigger emotion in any given situation. Behavioral methods are often used to accomplish this task and education components are often coupled with client homework for successful treatment,"[28] (emphasis mine).

Here's what I've learned. You shape your "interpretation and construction of (a) situation" from

- the influence of authority figures (parents, teachers, coaches, others).
- your family of origin (parents, grandparents, siblings, cousins).
- childhood wounds (which likely come from those mentioned above).

Thus you create your own realities and conclusions as to how life works. Through repetition of those early experiences, you form your self-reality. You see all of life through the lens of how *you* subconsciously *say* life works.

So it's not quite as simple as the rookie motivational speaker makes it seem by saying something like, "A thought creates a feeling, a feeling creates an emotion, and an emotion creates a behavior." That implies you can change everything with a single thought. A thought is not neutral, though. You give *meaning* to your thoughts based on how you see life and yourself in that life experience or event. And often those meanings can be skewed.

And most of us see life through a haze. And (unfortunately) it will be like that until we see Jesus.

For now we see in a mirror dimly, but then face to face. Now I know in part; then I shall know fully, even as I have been fully known (1 Corinthians 13:12, ESV).

Paul is saying that you may think you see well, but it is only a dim reflection of the final reality we will have in heaven

1. Pray and ask the Father for the right person for you.
2. Call several of the largest churches in your area to ask for recommendations.
3. Ask people you trust.
4. When you have some candidate counselors, ask each for references — people he or she has helped with issues similar to yours.
5. Go with an open mind for two to four sessions. Get a feel for the process.
6. Face your fear of opening up and take the risk.
7. Trust God.

You or your loved one don't have to live this way anymore. It will take time, but it's worth it.

> *"Self-sabotage is when we say we want something and then go about making sure it doesn't happen."*
> — Alyce P. Cornyn-Selby[29]

CHAPTER 9
EXPOSURE

"Vulnerability is not weakness...I define vulnerability as emotional risk, exposure, uncertainty. It fuels our daily lives."
— Dr. Brené Brown[30]

In this journey toward mental health, one of your greatest needs is to accept the reality of your shortcomings. Until then, you will not be able to make any real steps towards wellness.

We expose ourselves every day. After we shower, we get right to work exposing things! I lean into the mirror as I'm shaving. I make sure to get the eyebrows and nose hairs trimmed. Then I look closer to see how much hair is sticking out of my ears! To do that, I usually need a flashlight.

Meanwhile, my dear wife is practically *sitting* on the sink to get as close as she can to the mirror. She inspects all the nooks and crannies of her face, follicles, and eyelashes! Yes, we are meticulous about looking perfect before we leave the house.

Why aren't we this relentless about inspecting what keeps us in bondage, discouragement, or depression? Why aren't we this habitual about incorporating spiritual growth disciplines to keep us on track?

PRACTICE MAKES PERFECT?

You have heard that saying, but it's not necessarily true. If you are practicing incorrectly, then it is all for naught because the performance will be weak. To perform correctly, you must practice correctly.

Vocally, I never did. In college, I took one vocalization class, and it was very helpful. But since baseball was my priority—and I had enough natural singing talent to get by—I skipped additional vocal classes and sang without training until age thirty-three.

Then I began to lose my voice. At first I could not sustain the high notes. Then my range started to drop until I had difficulty sustaining an E flat above middle C. Simply put, I am a tenor, and a trained low bass can sing that note all day long. Sensing disaster, I called a friend in the music department at the University of Maryland. He gave me the names of two excellent voice teachers and recommended either.

The first one I called, Phyllis Joyce, had an opening that week. Six weeks later, I was my old self. A mere three months after our first lesson, I was hitting notes with regularity that I had only known a decade earlier even on my best days! Today I sing with ease in my sixties, all as a result of three-plus years with Phyllis's expertise.

During one of our early sessions, Phyllis and I discussed how most teachers instruct you to sing from your diaphragm. She wasted no time in correcting me. "It is incomplete advice. We don't sing from our diaphragm; we sing from our knees!" She went on to explain that even the foundation block of a house is built on the foundation footer. The footer makes contact with the ground, the bedrock, and it is leveled so that the foundation block is level too. It is the same with the diaphragm, for which your thighs, buttocks, and midsection are the foundation footer. When you understand this, you have an even stronger foundation to make vocal music. The diaphragm is free to be strong and support the flow of sound.

Phyllis then gave me four different diaphragm-strengthening exercises. With each repetition, I began to sing with breath control and volume I'd never known. It was liberating.

To keep me from slipping into bad habits, Phyllis had me practice in front of a mirror as often as possible. That way I could see the placement of my vowels in pronunciation. I would know if my shoulders moved during breathing (they shouldn't). I could track my lungs and diaphragm (tl should expand rather than move up and down) — and so on.

The best place for this was the powder room. It was small, had a nice-sized mirror, and echoed wonderfully so that I could see and hear everything that was good and not so good about my singing. The powder room was all about exposure.

It is essential for you to find your areas of exposure. Your metaphorical powder room will likely be a person who can give you honest feedback on what others see that you don't. That way, you can stay "in tune."

So where do you go to make corrections in your life? Later we will go more in depth on this, but for now know you must lay yourself bare before God and your family. They already know what your issues are; they're just waiting for you to ask for help.

BEGIN WITH CONFESSION…

If we confess our sins, he is faithful and just and will forgive us our sins and purify us from all unrighteousness (I John 1:9).

Admit your faults to one another and pray for each other so that you may be healed (James 5:16, TLB).

Regarding honesty about sin, the Bible also says, *"Whoever conceals their sins does not prosper, but the one who confesses and renounces them finds mercy"* (Proverbs 28:13).

The word *confess* simply means "to agree." When you confess your sins to God, you agree to what He says about them. You don't qualify or justify them. You just say, "God, I have broken Your law by (fill in the blank), and I'm guilty. I receive Your forgiveness by faith and thank You for restoring me to fellowship with You." That's it. And when you truly accept His forgiveness (and this sometimes involves forgiving yourself), you have a conscience set free to move forward.

I remember returning from a counseling session in the fall of 1979. Still dealing with the guilt of going AWOL from my first ministry assignment to Europe, I flipped through a stack of scripture cards for memorization purposes. I came to Hebrews 9:14 – *"How much more shall the blood of Christ, who through the eternal Spirit offered himself without spot to God, purge your conscience from dead works to serve the living God?"* (KJV).

The words "purge your conscience" leaped off that card and into my heart! I pulled off the road and wept with pure joy at the thought of God really and truly forgiving me for walking out on Him. I still recall that time as a pivot point in my spiritual journey.

Just as God exposes your failings to bring you to a place of repentance, this same God often gives you one person with whom to share yourself. If you are fortunate enough to find this life partner, he/she forms a crucial part of your healing process.

That last sentence may make single readers uneasy. I don't want you to think that you are somehow irretrievable just because you're not married. As you will read, marriage comes with its own set of challenges if you are not mature enough.

I believe one of the reasons for the prevalence of divorce, even among Christians, is because of the revealing exposure that is intrinsically created. I know every relationship is different, but the following generalization has elements of truth for us all.

While you are dating someone, both of you are trying your best. You'll make the extra effort to present yourself favorably, and so will your partner. You want to sell him/her on a better version of who or what you really are! We all do this.

Even if you live together in sin (i.e., without marriage), you and your partner do not totally expose yourselves. Unconsciously, you might put off marriage because you care for this person too much to let him/her see who you really are.

After marriage, you both experience a natural relaxing of your guard. Your real self comes out, and most of the time it's not pretty. She has not applied the emotional makeup. His face is all-rough with a two-day-old relational beard. In short, you are exposed.

Then, usually, you or your spouse will demand that the other must change. Can you imagine demanding that a mirror change its reflection? In reality, you can't take your own self-exposure because you don't have the emotional maturity. So you blame the other and eventually run.

It has been like that from the beginning. When Adam and Eve first sinned (Genesis 3:6-13), "then the eyes of both of them were opened, and they realized they were naked (exposed); so they sewed fig leaves together (grabbing for options) and made coverings for themselves (avoiding reality)."

That was not bad enough. When God called for them ("Where are you?"), His question was not for information. He knew exactly where they were; He wanted them to admit their reality. Their responses are telling.

Adam: "I heard you in the garden, and I was afraid because I was naked so I hid." (I'm fearful of exposure.)

God: "Who told you that you were naked? Have you eaten from the tree that I commanded you not to eat from?" (God is demanding accountability.)

Adam: "The woman You put here with me she gave me some fruit from the tree and I ate it." (Adam avoids accountability and finds someone else to blame—God and Eve.)

God (to Eve): "What is this you have done?" (Accountability again.)

Eve: "The serpent deceived me, and I ate" (I did it, but it's his fault...half-admittance.)

(The first couple remained together despite losing their beautiful home in Eden. But this may have been from the lack of alternatives!)

Marriage is unique among relationships in how it exposes you to the realities of your shortcomings.

As we prepared to move out of the home that Alicia loved into a rental that was very disappointing to her, I began to go into my typical depressive and negative self-talk.

The biggest struggle that Alicia has had through the years with me has been my negativity and the rehearsing of Murphy's Law ("if anything can go wrong, it will") when things were challenging. I started in with the negativity as we were driving down the road. Alicia lost it. She was completely out of character and began beating the dashboard and screaming how frustrated she was with my "total preoccupation with myself" and not coming through as a team player with tasks that I needed to do involving the move. I felt sorry for myself and didn't hurt for her and what she was going through.

I completely understood her outrage and frustration, but of course, this only pushed me further into shame and self-loathing. It was around this time that Alicia began to wonder if she had made a mistake twenty-nine years earlier in marrying me. She thought to herself, "Tim and I have none of the same goals. I want to move forward in life and he wants to move backwards."

It was at that time that she found my counselor Bob at the recommendation of one of her friends. She used the time to vent to him and allowed him to be the one to confront me. It gave her hope knowing that when things would bother her she didn't need to speak with me about it. She knew she could tell Bob and let him take care of my dysfunctional cognitive thinking.

Could Alicia have handled this incident better? Perhaps if she were Mother Theresa she could have! But we all have our breaking point and the pressure for her had finally hit.

Another tipping point came in 2013 when Alicia's frustration level peaked. It had been three-and-a-half years since I was gainfully employed. She was exasperated. She had put up with so much. She was still living without hopes and goals for our future and was angry and heartbroken. For our other four kids she was home every night, with family dinners, and conversation around the table. I had made a commitment that I would cook, do homework, and spend time with Naomi while Alicia was out earning income, but I didn't follow through. Through tears she yelled at me over the loss of time with our daughter in her middle school years.

But it was during those middle school years when I was at my worst and lowest points; I didn't have the emotional energy to function, let alone be a good dad. She was angry because she believed that I could just turn on a switch and be happy, "think differently," be responsible and productive. In some ways depression can be as tough on the family as the depressive.

Why did our marriage survive and others' don't? I don't have that answer. Other than God's sovereign work of grace on our behalf, I don't know why we are still together and actually happy and in love today! But I do know that there are certain components that have to be present in a lasting relationship. I think we have to:

1. Ask "What will be the fallout of dissolving this marriage?" When David slept with Uriah's wife Bathsheba and then murdered her husband, one of the consequences of his sin was listed in II Samuel 12:14, "...*By this deed you have given occasion to the enemies of the Lord to blaspheme...*" (NASB). As a believer I have to ask myself, often, "Am I more concerned about my perceived happiness or God's holiness in my life?"
2. Ask "How will this affect my children, grandchildren, and our legacy?"
3. Make a commitment to commitment. When we said our vows "Till death do us part" we both meant it. (Only once has Alicia said, "I didn't say anything about murder!")
4. Call forth the emotional determination to take the humble step away from blaming and toward improvement. Then you can truly experience the beauty of forgiveness and reconciliation.

Can one come face to face with their own yet-to-be-revealed issues without marriage? Can a single person radically grow, endure exposure, and experience as well as extend forgiveness and reconciliation? Absolutely. It will just happen another noble way (God does "everything well" [Mark 7:37]). It will require more intentionality to seek out platonic relationship(s) that will facilitate accountable growth. And God, because He is "for us and not against us," will provide this because, remember…"He will provide."

As iron sharpens iron, so one person sharpens another (Proverbs 27:17).

My son, Ivan, is currently working, studying, and involved in living out the Great Commission in the Orlando area. As he waits on God's choice for a mate, he doesn't let that distract him from his current calling. He is proactive in making relationships so he can grow emotionally and relationally. He has a core group of friends that he is doing life with and he is growing in the Lord.

I have a forty-eight-year-old male friend in south Florida who is content as a single servant of the Lord. He's played piano in the same church since age fourteen and rarely takes vacations because he feels so fulfilled. God has given him purpose and meaningful relationships in his church and school family. He is a gift to the body of Christ.

I had a sixty-four year old friend, "John" who was married for over twenty years to an amazing, godly woman (her second marriage) and step children who loved him, but…

He died from "failure to thrive" (FTT), which is almost always a condition diagnosed in children. His depression literally took his life. Why? He refused to eat or to speak to those closest to him because of his self-imposed shame over several business and professional failures.

Another friend of mine, "Kent" was in professional ministry but struggled with the sin of sexual addiction that cost him his marriage. Some close friends and I became his recovery team and I thought we were going to lose him once to suicide. He was on a high dose of Prozac and seeing a counselor weekly for several years. He was sure, at best, he would never remarry or "live" again, but did everything his recovery team asked of him and more. He went the extra mile to work on himself and restore his broken relationships. Today he's in a new marriage, has a new ministry, and is *so* in love with God for restoring him to fruitful and meaningful living.

Whether married or single, you must utilize the powder rooms and the mirrors of life. Listen to the sounds. View the sights. Embrace exposure both before your God and the primary people He places in your life. Then the tune of your life will grow closer to the right key and pitch.

CHAPTER 10

NO SOLOS ALLOWED

"Solitude is a chosen separation for refining your soul. Isolation is what you crave when you neglect the first."
— Wayne Cordeiro, *Leading on Empty: Refilling Your Tank and Renewing Your Passion*[31]

Have you opened up to anyone about your struggles with depression? Do you have someone, friend or family, with whom you can share the tough stuff of your life?

If this has been a lifelong, losing battle, my guess is no. Our natural inclination during depression is isolation. Tell me, does this sound familiar?

- "I can't share this with my friend. He's going through his own issues."
- "I've tried to share before...and got nothing but judgment!"
- "When I tried to open up, I got sympathy but little help."
- "If I share this misery, my spouse will resent me and think she does not fulfill me. She might even leave me."
- "Even if I do share how I feel, it won't help...nothing will."

And perhaps most common in the Christian community:

- "I can't open up; I'm supposed to be the example of Christ and live in joy. How will anyone be able to follow me? I am a failure in ministry and everyone will judge me."

Are these thoughts familiar to you? This may be what you think, but let me assure you it is not reality.

These are flawed assumptions. They come from erroneous reasoning that keeps you stuck in your emotional prison. Thus you lose your power to proactively work toward getting out.

You may have experienced judgment. Or maybe you got sympathy without help. That simply means you were with the wrong person. You must seek out other people who will listen, empathize, and offer encouragement. Maybe even someone you haven't met yet.

So know this: you are not alone.

STRENGTH IN NUMBERS

I will never forget my first church solo. I was fourteen, singing in a teen ensemble. After we sang the first verse and chorus as a group, I would take the microphone, step forward, and sing verse two. I was *petrified*, but I survived. A few months later, I graduated to a real solo—all alone on the platform.

A lady came up to me afterward and said, "My, my, young man, you have such wonderful vibrato for your age!"

I replied, "Thank you, Ma'am, but that wasn't vibrato; that was nerves!"

Eventually four of us decided to form a teen vocal quartet. Three of us were becoming accomplished soloists, but we truly enjoyed the camaraderie. We learned to blend our voices through different parts and arrangements as we pooled our vocal resources. We got better as people and musicians, which in turn made us better soloists.

Interestingly, the church music director who had put us together was also assembling other teen groups in the church: two trios, another ensemble, and several duets. Out of an eighty-voice church choir, we had about twenty teens. *Twenty* of us *mentored* by some sixty adult voices three times weekly. No wonder many of us have gone on to successful music ministry careers.

I think you see my point. Even a soloist cannot succeed on his own. We need others—friends, relatives, teachers, coaches, and "fellow strugglers and travelers." We are all on a journey toward personal growth and wholeness. You may get to a place where you can, when called on, go it alone. But the norm is community.

Jesus Himself set this example. He asked His friends to be with Him on the night His betrayal loomed—the night He experienced spiritual and mental anguish beyond what we can ever imagine.

> *Then Jesus went with his disciples to a place called Gethsemane, and he said to them, "Sit here while I go over there and pray." He took Peter and the two sons of Zebedee along with him, and he began to be sorrowful and troubled. Then he said to them, "My soul is overwhelmed with sorrow to the point of death. **Stay here and keep watch with me**"* (Matthew 26:36–38, emphasis mine).

When Jesus was at His lowest point, he wanted—needed—people to be with Him. We do too.

Look around you. Who are the people in your life you can trust? I guarantee you they are closer than you think. They are also probably aware, at least a little, of your troubles. They are only waiting for an invitation to come alongside you and pray with you. They want to minister to you, share your burden, and love you. Remember the words of Paul from Galatians 6:2: *"Carry each other's burdens, and in this way you will fulfill the law of Christ."*

The Christian life allows no solos. We are a body and community that should take care of one another. Don't let pride, fear, and flawed thinking rob you of receiving aid, or rob others of the blessing of serving you as a brother or sister. God will use people around us to give us hope, which is what we depressives need the most. Hope anticipates that something will change—circumstances, finances, or *something*. A small ray of hope will break through your storm clouds and restore the smile of your soul if only for five minutes.

STATISTICAL REALITIES

"Tim, three months ago our pastor was diagnosed as bi-polar."

I was introducing my concert ministry to "Peter," a church music director. A cold call such as this usually follows the same pattern—initial pleasantries, networking ("so-and-so suggested I give you a call"), name-dropping ("I used to sing on *In Touch TV* with Dr. Charles Stanley"), leaving website information, emailing music samples, and scheduling a follow-up call. (I am so thankful that Alicia does most of this. I loathe the phone—it's part of my fear of rejection.) I also try to be transparent, briefly mentioning my three depressions. The whole call generally takes about five minutes.

For Peter, the word *depression* extended the conversation to thirty-five minutes! He shared with me how his pastor, "Victor," had been unsteady for almost a year. Victor would have outbursts of anger during staff meetings followed by periods of sullenness and escape. The staff would cover for him until his actions finally indicated he might hurt himself. Peter called the state denomination board for intervention.

Victor went on medication for three months. He seemed to be stabilizing but was still not vocationally functional. So Victor had to resign and get further help. This caused a new despair so that he was still in danger of suicide. He was at that place that Bob, my counselor, described as "coming out of the curve." Here's how Bob explains it:

> *Tim, imagine an inverted bell curve with a downward slope. Some think that it is when the person is at their lowest – at the bottom of the curve – that they are in danger of committing suicide. But it's actually when a person is starting on the upward slope that they are most in danger of taking their life. No longer feeling totally helpless, their reasoning returns. They are able to assess where they've*

been and often they surmise, "This is too tough. There's too much work involved. I don't want to hope again, just to be disappointed again. Nothing will ever change." As they plot and imagine their own demise, the process begins to take on a life of its own. This is when friends, family members and professionals need to be extra vigilant and tuned in to the depressive's "progress."

Per Peter's description of the situation, Victor wasn't at his *lowest* point but just above it, where most suicides take place.

My curiosity began to grow, so I searched the Internet for "pastors," "suicide," and "USA statistics." Article after article came up: pastoral suicide, pastoral depression, pastoral burnout, and depression in ministerial families. Here is just a sampling:

There is no lack of statistics about pastors and depression, burnout, health, low pay, spirituality, relationships and longevity – and none of them are good. According to the Schaeffer Institute, seventy percent of pastors constantly fight depression, and seventy-one percent are burned out. Meanwhile, seventy-two percent of pastors say they only study the Bible when they are preparing for sermons; and eighty percent believe pastoral ministry has negatively affected their families.[32]

So seventy percent are constantly fighting depression?

Thom Rainer, president and CEO of LifeWay Christian Resources, states that in the top five problems pastors face, numbers three, four, and five are stress, depression, and burnout.[33]

Then, these two *telling* statistics:

- Fifty-six percent of pastors' wives say that they have no close friends.[34]
- Seventy percent of pastors don't have any close friends.[35]

- Hmmm...interesting correlation: seventy percent of pastors "constantly fight depression," and the same percentage don't have any close friends.

A recent Duke University study revealed a phenomenon that will not surprise those of us in vocational ministry, but it may shock the rest of you. The title of the news release said it all: "Clergy More Likely to Suffer from Depression, Anxiety."[36]

The study, published in the *Journal of Primary Prevention*, compared the mental health of ninety-five percent of the United Methodist clergy in North Carolina (1,176 pastors) to a representative sample of Americans. Conclusion?

> *The demands placed on clergy by themselves and others put pastors at far greater risk for depression than individuals with other occupations. "Greater" as in double the national rate.*[37]

You may be asking, "Tim, I don't want to be insensitive here, but why are you sharing stats regarding pastors? That's not my profession."

My points are the following:

1. Pastors and counselors have studied and prepared to be professional people-helpers. So we perceive they should be almost statistically exempt from depression. Because they see the issues so clearly in others, they should be able to see them in themselves.
2. Therefore pastors and counselors have walked in your shoes and can be a trusted resource for you.
3. One large church in my network has over ten pastors on staff. Half of them are on some form of anti-depressant. Most of the pastors' wives are on anti-depressant or antianxiety medication.
4. Pray daily for your pastor and/or counselor. They carry a heavy burden.

These stats of people in the people-helping business prompted me to then look at the general population. After consulting several websites (CDC, NIH, and such), I found the following:

According to depression statistics from the Centers for Disease Control and Prevention (CDC), about nine percent of adult Americans have feelings of hopelessness, despondency, and/or guilt that generate a diagnosis of depression. At any given time, about three percent of adults have major depression, also known as major depressive disorder (MDD), a long-lasting and severe form of depression. In fact, major depression is the leading cause of disability for Americans between the ages of fifteen and forty-four, according to the CDC.[38]

Nine percent of adults in the USA—that's almost thirty million people! Out of any ten people you work with, one battles depression. Likewise with any ten individuals with whom you attend church or ten people you pass in the mall, at the beach, or anywhere.

And whether they are pastors, Christian, atheists, Muslim, Jewish, blue collar, white collar, or whatever, one of the common denominators is *isolation*.

Per WebMD research writer Jennifer Soong, the top depression trap to avoid is social withdrawal.

"When we're clinically depressed, there's a very strong urge to pull away from others and to shut down," says Stephen Ilardi, PhD, author of the book The Depression Cure, *and associate professor of psychology at the University of Kansas. "It turns out to be the exact opposite of what we need...In depression, social isolation typically serves to worsen the illness and how we feel," Ilardi says. "Social withdrawal amplifies the brain's stress response. Social contact helps put the brakes on it."[39]*

However, we do our absolute best to avoid people when depressed.

- The spiritual person thinks, "I can't let anyone know because I'm supposed to have it together. My faith is supposed to be the difference maker."
- The ashamed person thinks, "If I open up and get real, he may not stick around."
- The sensitive person thinks, "I can't share this with her; she has problems of her own."
- The hopeless person thinks, "Even if I do share, it won't make any difference. He can't help anyway."
- The angry person thinks, "She will just judge me. No way am I opening up to *her*!"

And on it goes. But notice the common factor in each statement above: "The (fill in the blank) person thinks." We try to go it alone. We try to solo our way out of our depression.

Remember that old adage, "there's strength in numbers." You don't get better on your own. You need others. As Barbara Streisand used to sing, "People who need people are the luckiest people in the world."

But shame, embarrassment, and sadness keep us from stepping out.

- You're ashamed to be around people because "they know" or "they may find out."
- You're embarrassed to have your weakness exposed. You don't have it together, either as much as you thought or as much as you tried to portray — or both.
- You're too sad to go out. You don't want to bring others down. You can't pretend to be happy when called upon. You just don't have the energy for it.

So, you avoid people. You hide, literally. Me? I would sleep on the couch or go to Starbucks, spending money we didn't have on the most expensive coffee on the planet! I'd read the paper or books—anything to avoid engaging with people.

An important component of my healing came from my dear wife sticking by me. She would ask me to take her out to eat. This was not to avoid meal prep (she has a black-belt in cooking!) but to get me out in public, around people—even people we didn't know. She would have friends "drop by"— friends aware of my issues and wanting to help. Plus, we went to church. A few people knew "something's not quite right with Tim," but staying involved musically in our home church was, and continues to be, a large part of the healing, maintenance, and growth process.

FORMING YOUR OWN "ENSEMBLE"

I've always prayed this prayer: "Lord, bring into my life the right books, CDs, DVDs, podcasts, Scripture passages, other resources, people, teachers, and whatever I need to stay on track with You. I know I can trust You to meet these needs for my continued growth and maturation in Christ." And He has answered that prayer again and again.

So how do you form your own ensemble of people to help you fend off the tendency toward isolation?

1. Pray that prayer to ask the Lord to help you specifically in this regard.
2. If you are single, join a singles' group. Ask for recommendations from large churches (usually well networked in communities), counselors, and other singles.
3. If you are married, join a couples' group or "life group" (the new word for "Sunday School class"). Again, get references from other couples and counselors at large churches.
4. Guys, join a men's group. I'm part of one, and it is rich and necessary for all of us. Oh, the issues and stories…

5. Ladies, join a ladies' Bible study. Alicia meets weekly with seven other women to pray and do studies by Beth Moore, Priscilla Shirer, and the like.

Both Alicia and I can tell you that what takes place in these respective groups will change your life! This kind of contact and fellowship refreshes the soul. God has wired us to seek true community, but the Fall has warped our thinking toward isolation.

Someone has said, "You can't steer a car unless it's moving, and God can't direct your life unless you are moving too." I agree.

Take the risk to start somewhere. Remember Jesus said:

Ask and it will be given to you; seek and you will find; knock and the door will be opened to you. For everyone who asks receives; the one who seeks finds; and to the one who knocks, the door will be opened (Matthew 7: 7–8).

His instruction involves a word we don't like much—process. Asking is step one. (Ask friends and churches for recommendations). Then we have to seek (evaluate potential support groups and counselors). Finally, we knock. (You must actually *go* to that group meeting or therapy appointment!) Throughout it you must trust God with the outcome. The point is, we *engage*.

If your depressive loved one is anything like I was, they can't or won't do this alone. So you need to get them up off of the couch and into someplace with a crowd like a concert or professional sports event. Then go to a restaurant with people of all ages and long lines waiting to get in. Go to church and hear the truth (even the uncomfortable truth) spoken in love and grace.

Then go to a movie with a group of friends. Meet up afterward at a café or coffee shop to discuss the film.

Make some of the calls they can't make…to counselors or group therapy sessions. Let them know what you've found out or "heard about" said counselor or group.

Finally, continue talking daily. Check in on your depressive loved one; find out how they are doing and their plans for the coming days.

Don't go it alone; no solos allowed.

CHAPTER 11
CAMARADERIE OF THE CHOIR

"Alone we can do so little, together we can do so much."
—Helen Keller [40]

You can accomplish very few goals alone. Any musical or stage production needs a large team to succeed. Besides the actors and musicians you can see, it takes lighting and sound crew, directors, writers, producers, promo, and publicity personnel, and others. A successful organization will have a competent CEO and management team. Even in war, ground and naval units work together with air support. All have their distinct roles. Each has a different skill but has the same objective: to win.

I do not know if I would be here without the people God placed in my life. In this journey toward mental health, one of your greatest needs is exposure to the reality of your shortcomings. Until you can see yourself clearly, flaws and all, you will not be able to make any real steps towards wellness. Trust me when I tell you God will reveal people in your life who will expose to you the specific areas you need to tackle on your road to wellness.

Here are a few of my "choir members" — key people that have helped me achieve harmony and wholeness.

KEY PEOPLE – SPIRITUAL GUIDE

The first person who lifted me up was the pastor who led my parents to the Lord. When I came home from the mission field in 1979, I was defeated. Pastor Fitz gave me a job, a place to live, and time to recover. Yes, this was part of his profession as a minister, but he had also suffered depression in his Bible college years. He had to drop out for over a semester. He had been where I was; he knew how the depressive thinks, feels, and acts. Thus he knew well how to minister to those like me. That was a season of rest, recovery, and growth for me, and, as God would have it in His providence, it led me to the person who has encouraged me the most over the years, my wife.

KEY PEOPLE – LIFE PARTNER

Alicia grew up in a broken home. Much younger than her siblings, she was essentially an only child. From age six, she was a "latchkey kid," staying at home alone after school until her mom got home from work, sometimes as late as nine. My mother-in-law, exhausted and fighting her own emotional demons, gave Alicia little time.

Alicia and I began dating in the summer of 1980 and married in February of 1981. I remember a conversation from the fall of 1980 when a tearful Alicia said, "I'm just so tired of being alone."

Two lonely and needy people found each other. How grateful I am that she has been a continual help to me.

It is not good for the man to be alone. I will make a helper suitable for him (Genesis 2:18).

I couldn't ask for a better match. Though Alicia was only nineteen when we married, she exhibited phenomenal wisdom and grace. When I could only hear, "not good enough, never have enough," Alicia literally prayed my first album into reality. She stayed home and raised five kids, often as a "single" parent. Sometimes I was away forty to fifty weekends a year.

When I would sabotage our finances, she educated herself in real estate and business marketing. As I mentioned earlier, our family stayed afloat because of her.

When we sold her dream house, she squared her shoulders and found a rental house. She made it a home with little help from me (enmeshed in a full-blown depressive episode).

Through all of that, she spoke the truth in love (Ephesians 4:15) and never disparaged me to others, including our children. She still respected me as the head of the household even when I failed her as a leader. God blessed me abundantly when He chose Alicia as my bride.

KEY PEOPLE – HONEST AND TRUSTWORTHY FRIENDS

The Father has also been faithful to provide the right friends in the right moments. One of those friends would call to either walk a couple of miles or meet at the gym to work out. Yes, we benefited physically, but his motivation was to get me out of the house and engage interpersonally.

I have several friends willing to answer my calls anytime. Knowing my whole story, they're actually glad to hear from me!

Often times, we as depressives are so consumed with ourselves and problems that we haven't developed the "muscle" of friend making. We have to "exercise" and engage in a new "workout" so that we can find the people to be with in this kind of relationship.

This solution may take a little time, but the Bible says, "*A man who has friends must himself be friendly*" (Proverbs 18:24, NKJV). To make friends we have to be a friend. A short book on how to reach out to others is *Skill with People* by Les Giblin. Let me encourage you to make this part of your personal growth exercise and, as you read, journal the names of a person or two whom you could be friendly with, who, in turn, will possibly become a "friend who sticks closer than a brother" (or sister), which is the second half of Proverbs 18:24!

Another friend of mine failed in his marriage and almost committed suicide. Then he made an amazing, grace-filled comeback. Our talks are authentic, honest, and renewing. We can share anything, and that is liberating. He makes a point to call me weekly. What a blessing to have a close friendship.

A word of caution whether you are married or single...if you are female look for this kind of relationship with other females and if you are a man, seek out a brother for this kind of relationship.

> *As iron sharpens iron, so one person sharpens another,* (Proverbs 27:17).

KEY PEOPLE – SMALL GROUPS

In some seasons, you may need a group setting to move toward healing. Your counselor will know if you need a small group, and he/she may even recommend one. Since visiting a group one time does not constitute a commitment, you should sample a variety before settling on one. If your therapist has a group and invites you in, that's ideal. The group can become an integral part of your treatment. This will hasten your growth and healing.

A word of caution: groups are usually for a season. Do not feel slighted if someone leaves the group or guilty if you need to leave a group. Some last only weeks or months. Others can extend for years. Give and receive in the group. Remember, the others are hurting like you; just as you need their input, they need yours. Try to listen more than talk.

I have been in a number of groups. One group, "the Nexus," worked well for several months. But then we hit a plateau, and I knew I had to move on. I announced I would start a new group in four weeks, and I hoped the Nexus would remain intact and take on a new member. The entire Nexus membership looked at me in disbelief. They felt abandoned. After I left, the Nexus carried on for only about six more weeks. It saved one member's marriage, and I'm grateful for that.

Perhaps you know someone ashamed, depressed, or just beat up by life. He/she has hit hard times, like so many have today. He/she likely wants to change this situation but needs temporary help. Maybe you can be the one to supply that need.

A word to the wise: Every now and then, you will meet people with the "victim mentality." They relish in receiving perpetual help. When you offer help, you become something of an enabler. But I believe this problem is rare.

Choirs have tenors, sopranos, altos, and basses. They have men and women—young, old, and middle-aged. All contribute uniquely toward the harmony and beauty of the song. And just as a choir needs all of those parts and people, we need different people in our lives to stay in tune. We will present our best song when we intentionally incorporate these components into our lives.

Oh! And don't forget to be a member of someone else's choir. What "part" do you bring to their song?

CHAPTER 12
TOOLS OF THE TROUPE

"I'm going to use all my tools, my God-given
ability, and make the best life I can with it."
— LeBron James

Watch any rock band, actors' troupe, or traveling ensemble set up, and you will see tool after tool coming in from a van, bus or eighteen-wheeler!

Dollies and hand trucks bring speakers, anvil cases, light bars, mixing boards, and more — or sometimes it's sheer old-fashioned, back-breaking, over-the-shoulder carry-ins! A three-hour show usually takes eight to ten hours of setup, testing, troubleshooting, retesting before the curtain comes up. Then after the show the teardown begins another multi-hour ordeal of disassembly and load out.

Most of us need a computer today. But not just a computer; we need a jump drive and/or an external hard drive in addition to a cloud account for backup. We integrate our phones, tablets, and other devices with said computer. Some of us travel with mini-printers or scanners because they are indispensable to our work.

Tools of the troupe — or trade.

Remember that prayer a few chapters back? "Lord, bring into my life the right people, books, podcasts, CDs, DVDs, messages, films, phone calls, Scripture, and anything else that will help me walk not only with You but help me to walk more like You; those things that will help me grow as a person of faith." When you pray thus, you really pray for tools to help you find and stay on the pathway of your faith journey with Him. Your challenge, like mine, is to educate yourself and utilize the tools He provides. Because — remember: "He will provide." We already covered that, right?

OUR TOOLS - SCRIPTURE

Scripture is the book we turn to first. Psalms 119:130 says,

The entrance of Your words gives light; it gives understanding to the simple (NKJV).

When depressed, you may often describe your life as "in the dark." St. John of the Cross wrote centuries ago that his experience was his "dark night of the soul."

To give your soul comfort and perspective, spend time in the Bible—in particular, the book of Psalms. King David wrote most of the Psalms and battled intense discouragement and disappointment with God. The Psalms are full of honest wrestling with God, who does not condemn David for this. In fact, He seems to say, "Bring it on." This does not mean you should disrespect Him, but remember that one of His names is "Wonderful Counselor," (Isaiah 9:6). He is quite secure in who He is, and He *"pities* (has compassion on) *those who fear Him,"* (Psalms 103:13).

(The Lord) does not punish us for all our sins; He does not deal harshly with us, as we deserve. For His unfailing love toward those who fear Him is as great as the height of the heavens above the earth. He has removed our sins as far from us as the east is from the west. The Lord is like a father to his children, tender and compassionate to those who fear Him. For He knows how weak we are; He remembers we are only dust. Our days on earth are like grass; like wildflowers, we bloom and die. The wind blows, and we are gone – as though we had never been here. But the love of the Lord remains forever with those who fear Him (Psalms 103:10-17a, NLT).

Early in 2010, I probably didn't read my Bible for three months. I couldn't pick it up. Nothing was wrong with the Bible, just with me. But God didn't condemn; He waited. And when I finally did read it again—how fresh it was! How good it tasted!

If this is where you are, unable to read His word, God supplies other tools to get you back to where He is taking you.

OUR TOOLS – PRAYER

I will tell you from experience that one of the simplest prayers that God hears and answers is "God help me." During that three months I couldn't read my Bible, I could only pray—and only those three words.

I could not pray for my wife, kids, provision, or others—let alone the noble causes of need around the world. I could not express praise or gratitude. All I could pray was, "God help me." He is close to the brokenhearted.

- *There is no one like God…Who rides on the heavens to help you (Deuteronomy 33:26).*

- *He is your shield and helper (Deuteronomy 33:29).*

- *Hear my cry for help, my King and my God, for to You I pray (Psalms 5:2).*

- *For He has not despised or scorned the suffering of the afflicted one; He has not hidden His face from him but has listened to his cry for help (Psalms 22:24).*

- *Lord my God, I called to You for help, and You healed me (Psalms 30:2).*

- *I do believe; help me overcome my unbelief! (Mark 9:24).*

- *And I will ask the Father, and He will give you another Advocate to help you and be with you forever (John 14:6).*

- *Because He himself suffered when He was tempted, He is able to help those who are being tempted (Hebrews 2:18).*

- *Let us then approach God's throne of grace with confidence, so that we may receive mercy and find grace to help us in our time of need (Hebrews 4:16).*

Jesus meets you — not where you should be, but where you are. And that meeting has a purpose: to take you where you need to be, where you can again be joyful, productive, and helpful. So pray. Pray simply, pray what you can, and pray with the proverbial faith the size "of a grain of mustard seed." It is enough, because He is enough.

OUR TOOLS – PERSONAL JOURNAL

Do not misunderstand about journaling. Some liken it to a diary, and you may find some similarities. A journal can be regular, but more likely will be seasonal. My daughter Amber has battled her own times of darkness and anger towards God. She once filled seven journals within two years, but since then she's only felt the need to journal a few times a year.

A journal can take a multitude of forms. It is a record of the day's events and what they meant to you. Entries can be prayers, or you can outpour your feelings of betrayal and angst toward God. You could note the outside media you are utilizing as healing tools, or you could record your thoughts and feelings during therapy.

Craft this tool of journaling to your specific personality and needs. Just sit down and write. You will be amazed at how therapeutic this can be for your healing. Do not be afraid to share your writing with the people the Lord has sent alongside you. Be willing to bare your soul with transparency. One of the great benefits will be to one day look back and recount what God did in your dark hours. It will also be a record someday for your family to read after you are gone. You will leave a legacy to God's faithfulness.

OUR TOOLS – THE LOCAL CHURCH

I am so very grateful for the scripture that says *"And let us not neglect our meeting together, as some people do, but encourage one another, especially now that the day of His return is drawing near"* (Hebrews 10:25, NLT).

God in His perfect wisdom gave us instruction to meet (at least) weekly as the Body of Christ for mutual edification and worship. When we come together we are reminded that

- we are part of something larger than ourselves.
- we have our hearts and minds reminded of eternal truth.
- we connect (if we choose to) with others on the journey for encouragement.
- Christ is coming for us ("the day of His return is near").

If you have been hurt by a church, you were simply in the wrong church. Don't give up on church; it's God's primary way of reaching the world with the gospel, warts and all. As the old radio preacher, Dr. J. Vernon McGee, used to say, "Find a church where you hear the pages of the Bible turned often." That may mean you need to change churches, but God will provide the right place for you.

OUR TOOLS - GOOD BOOKS/GOOD PEOPLE

Motivational speaker Charles "Tremendous" Jones said, "The difference between the person you are today and the person you are a year from now is

1. the books you read, and
2. the people you meet."

I am grateful for a hunger to read. We need to read what others have to say.

I remember the first time I read *Disappointment with God* by Philip Yancey. I was very angry with the Father. This was right after the birth of our third child, Sophia.

We had prayed fervently as a family that Alicia would deliver safely. Even our five-year-old twins prayed with us. Of course, the Lord would answer their prayers, right?

Sophia was born two weeks late, her lungs full of meconium (the sticky fecal matter of a preborn in the confines of the womb). The doctors put her on life support and moved her to another hospital. After Alicia stabilized and Sophia improved from critical to serious, I went home for some rest and wrestled with God about what had transpired.

My phone rang. It was Bruce Peterson, a friend from Dallas. "Tim, I just heard the news. How are you?"

I proceeded to unload the truck! I told Bruce I was angry at God. But Bruce listened and began to minister from an understanding heart. You see, he had a son, Deron, who almost died from leukemia — twice, in fact. Bruce and his wife, Maggie, even planned his funeral. But Deron would survive to serve several terms on the foreign mission field, and he's still in ministry today.

He recommended *Disappointment with God*, and that book guided me through that season of anger. It has continued to minister to me over the years. For more recommendations on titles that helped me through dark times, see the suggested reading list.

Notice in this one instance, I

1. heard from a friend (good people) who
2. made a call, who recommended
3. a book (good books).

These two components will happen for you too as you pray and look for them.

OUR TOOLS – MEDIA/PODCASTS

Perhaps you are not a reader or writer, though. Thankfully, our God has other ways to reach out to you. Almost every type of media has ministered to me and shown me truth. My wife often starts her mornings listening to podcasts by various ministers. Personally, I listen to Ravi Zacharias or Tony Evans almost daily. Alicia listens almost daily to Joyce Meyer's podcast. The podcast tool has been such a blessing to help foster our continued spiritual growth.

OUR TOOLS – MEDIA/VIDEO

One of the tools available to us online is live streaming and/or video-casts. You can go to various helpful websites and get Bible study messages where the advantage is, you can pause and re-watch to take notes or, if interrupted, deal with whatever and then return and resume your study.

I remember a young lady with two very busy boys. When I asked her what she got from the pastor's message she replied, somewhat frustrated, "How would I know? I had to wrestle my two boys the whole time he was preaching!" That was over twenty years ago. Today, she could just go to her church website and re-watch the message.

DVDs can be ordered to watch and re-watch for in-depth study. One helpful resource is a video series by TV host and evangelist James Robison and his pastor, Robert Morris of Gateway Church near Ft. Worth, TX. It's called *Living Free* and can be ordered easily at Amazon or the Gateway Church website.

OUR TOOLS – MEDIA/FILM

Movies have spoken to me profoundly at times. I remember seeing *Saving Private Ryan*. Overwhelmed, I sat in the theater for at least twenty minutes while the credits rolled. I couldn't move from my seat; I was still taking in the sacrifice so many made during those terrible days of World War II.

However, no movie scene has moved me more than in the movie *Joseph*[41] (starring Ben Kingsley, Paul Mercurio, and Martin Landau). Sold into slavery by his treacherous brothers but now viceroy of Egypt, Joseph lays a trap to confront them with their past. Then he orders the guards to leave the room. He takes off his Egyptian headdress and announces that he, in fact, is Joseph. The brothers feel a shame eclipsed only by Joseph's forgiveness. Whenever I revisit the film, I sometimes watch the scene two or three times.

Your tools will open the door to speak to and with God. Depressives often feel as if they are praying to a brick wall. But you need only recognize that the Father provides you tools through books, podcasts, sermons, people, Scripture, and other media. Often those perceived walls begin to crumble, and you can once again come to the Throne of Grace.

He's willing to meet you where you are. Are you willing?

CHAPTER 13

STAYING IN TUNE

"Courage doesn't happen when you have all the answers. It happens when you are ready to face the questions you have been avoiding your whole life."
—Shannon L. Alder[42]

As important as family and friends are, they cannot be your only support system. Professional counseling is necessary to be able to navigate a true depressive's psyche. Perhaps the most important professional influence on my life is Jill. In August of 1991, I began to commute weekly from Orlando to Jacksonville to see her for three-hour sessions. At first I was apprehensive; Jill was female, charismatic, and Lutheran. All three of these aspects were far outside my faith tradition, but, as always, the Lord knows better than I. He provided the perfect asset for me.

By the end of session two, we were good friends. She understood me, and I had her help. Jill helped me discover my roots of bitterness toward my baseball coach and sixth grade teacher. She also pinpointed the lies I had lived by: "not good enough, never have enough."

On top of her wisdom and counseling insights, she pointed me toward invaluable resources, books, and recordings. Often the right people will know other right people, and most will know of the right book or other resource.

Many people, especially men, are reticent about opening up to a counselor. You might be afraid of seeming weak, flawed, or crazy![43]

So what? What if you're flawed? And what if you're just a little bit "crazy?" And what's so bad about admitting you're weak? The Bible says that's a good thing! About his painful and weakness-causing "thorn in the flesh," Paul wrote:

Three times I pleaded with the Lord to take it away from me. But he said to me, "My grace is sufficient for you, for my power is made perfect in weakness." Therefore I will boast all the more gladly about my weaknesses, so that Christ's power may rest on me. That is why, for Christ's sake, I delight in weaknesses, in insults, in hardships, in persecutions, in difficulties. For when I am weak, then I am strong (2 Corinthians 12:8–10).

OK, so we're weak. What about flawed? Are you flawed? Am I flawed? Yup!

*Let no one say when he is tempted, "I am being tempted by God" [for temptation does not originate from God, but from our own **flaws**]; for God cannot be tempted by [what is] evil, and He Himself tempts no one* (James 1:13, AMP, emphasis mine).

OK, we're weak and flawed. But what about crazy? Are we crazy? Sometimes.

*His messed-up, mixed-up children, his non-children, throw mud at him but none of it sticks. Don't you realize it is God you are treating like this? **This is crazy**; don't you have any sense of reverence? Isn't this your Father who created you, who made you and gave you a place on Earth?* (Deuteronomy 32:5–7, MSG, emphasis mine).

Since I'm weak, flawed, and sometimes "crazy" in the way I act or relate to God and others, I need regular checkups with my counselor—just as we need annual physicals and our cars need tune-ups.

Still, the risk is appreciable. Here are some things that have helped me open myself up to a new counselor:

- I categorized the counselor as a coach—someone trained in a particular area of specialization. A gymnastics coach will work with gymnasts as opposed to soccer players. A baseball hitting coach won't work with a quarterback. And it's the same with counselors. They specialize in human behavior and can help you get quickly to the root of your problems.
- The counselor is a skilled professional. Seek one with ten to twenty years of experience. He/she has likely seen your situation before and won't be guessing.
- The counselor is safe. Nothing will surprise him/her. He/she does not do shame and will keep your sessions private. (Licensed counselors must obey patient confidentiality laws. The only exception is if you reveal a crime or threats of harm to yourself or others.)

If you understand that you need the very help in which the counselor specializes, the counseling office is the one place you need to be. The experienced counselor can also spot whether you might need medication. Only a licensed psychiatrist or doctor can prescribe it (and only after a proper diagnosis), but a counselor can refer you.

Disclaimer: I am not a licensed medical professional, and you should take nothing in this chapter as medical advice. Consult a licensed health care provider before beginning any sort of medication or drug therapy.

Depending on the depth of your depression and the trauma you've experienced, a key ingredient in getting your song back may be drug therapy. Drugs create controversy, especially in Christian circles. Here is my simple and straightforward advice: if your doctor says take your medicine, take your medicine. Let others deal with the consequences.

Medication may be controversial, but it works. If you're going through trauma, a strong prescription can arrest a downward spiral. It can provide a season of relative calm so that you can begin healing.

When my daughter Amber was a freshman in college, she experienced a crisis of faith that sent her into a full-blown anxiety attack. While home for spring break, she lay nauseous in bed the entire time. She could not eat or sleep and lost weight. When she went back to school, she went to the doctor herself to get an antianxiety prescription. She experienced almost immediate clarity.

The root of her depression was some sin she needed to address. Once she had repented, a period of healing began, lasting about a year and a half. She was able to discontinue her medication after six months, and she has not needed it again since.

In my case, I had been on Zoloft from 2003 to early 2009. Then a well-meaning friend who had weaned himself from his medication persuaded me to do the same. I went off cold turkey without my doctor's input. That was not smart; lots of withdrawal issues. So I went back on the meds for a month, and then withdrew slowly this time but again, on my own without the help of my doctor.

It went fine until my January 2010 meltdown. As I write this, I am on two different meds. If I must remain on meds the rest of my life, I am good with that. And so is my family!

Another friend of mine "Mike," was a suicide candidate from late 1999 through 2000. Mike was on heavy medication for three years and then began to wean himself off with his doctor's supervision. Today Mike is free of all meds and succeeding as a church leader.

The point is that each one of us is different—in chemical makeup and circumstance. For the sake of our loved ones, you need to proceed prayerfully to do whatever is necessary to get well.

Many in the Christian culture believe you can achieve mental health through prayer and repentance only. Today we know too much about brain chemistry to make such a blanket assertion. Again, different people have different levels of serotonin. Medication can and does mitigate this chemical imbalance.

If your child broke his arm, would you deny him a visit to the doctor to set it and put it in a cast? Of course not! Why, then, would you deny medicine to a depressive?

Sometimes you can't accomplish total mental health through faith and prayer alone. Sometimes you need repentance too because certain sins manifest themselves in your depression. Likewise, medication is another tool you might need. For Amber, it supplied a clarity of mind that isolated her issues in a way she never could on her own. This topic may be way outside your comfort zone, but I adjure you not to cling to some perceived moral superiority. Your counselor and doctor will know whether to pursue this avenue.

POWER OF MEDICATIONS!

I will never forget my first experience with a drug, a 1992 steroid shot for a desperate shoulder pain. I'd been suffering for over a year, and my doctor finally gave me relief so that I could do physical therapy. When he put the needle in my shoulder, the instant it broke the skin, I started feeling better. I was stunned, and sobered. Drugs are amazingly powerful.

This power is, of course, problematic. So you always need to remain in close contact with your doctor during a drug treatment program.

As with most self-employed people, my business (or ministry) is "feast or famine" financially. Because some seasons generate more income than others, I have to plan for the leaner months. As the end of a tight month would approach and I knew the first of the month (bill-paying time) loomed, I would usually get agitated and short with my family. My anxiety would rise, and I'd experience mood swings. I learned later that this was an emotional "trigger point."

I went to my doctor, and he prescribed a medium dose of Zoloft for a couple of months. He informed me that my family might notice a change before I did.

After about three weeks, my wife was having a discussion with our twin daughters (seniors in high school at the time) in the family room. Alicia grew impatient, predicting I would be getting anxious about money and taking it out on them.

I stepped in. "Now, now, let's just relax and think this through. It isn't anything we haven't faced before. Let's just chill and find a solution."

In silence, the twins looked at each other, their mother, me, and then back at each other. Finally, Alexandra queried, "Who are you and what have you done with our parents? How is Dad the chill one in this situation?"

Alicia looked at me. "I guess the medicine is working."

Medication may be for a season. I have one friend, "Jason," who really messed up; he lost his marriage and ministry. At times, he turned suicidal. For a while, Jason was on strong medication. Today he has "graduated" from his meds and built a new ministry. On the other hand, medication may be a part of your routine for the rest of your life. Another friend of mine, "Pastor Curtis," grew afraid of going to the office. Is this really such an alien idea? Ministry is a high-pressure, high-stress job, including but not limited to spiritual care, funerals, comforting the bereaved, premarital counseling, church finances, and more. Curtis feared failing, despite an admirable track record. He shared that he felt as if he was sliding into a black hole.

After Curtis went to his doctor, he started medication. In less than three weeks, he could say, "I feel like myself again."

I asked him how long the prescription was.

His answer: "As long as it takes. If it's the rest of my life, so be it."

Another friend, "Hal," is the lead counselor of a megachurch. We were discussing the role of medication in the lives of people, including ministers. Hal said, "Tim we have a number of our staff who see a doctor regularly for their medication needs. Many of their wives are on medication as well. The pressures of ministry today are unprecedented. In fact, these days are the most troublesome I've seen in my thirty-plus years of ministry. You don't ever need to feel ashamed to be a minister on meds."

My dad first experienced a clinical depression while in the navy during the Korean War. He served four years stateside, married, and became a father. While he enjoyed playing basketball and fastpitch softball for the Great Lakes Naval Base teams, to this day, he is unsure what triggered the depression; nevertheless, it jumped up, grabbed him, and held on.

He managed until the summer of 1965. Burdened by his job and his parents' spiritual condition—they were not Christians at the time—he succumbed again. This time, it was an eight-month hospitalization that included eight shock treatments, hours of therapy, and medication.

His third clinical depression sneaked up and grabbed him again in the summer of 1986. Again, he required hospitalization. The doctors experimented with his meds over several months, and he began to settle down.

Since around 2001, he reports (and mom confirms) that he is emotionally fairly steady. He continues to see the doctor every few months. The current mix of meds seems to be working at age 88.

Dad prays every day for his kids and grandkids—just as he has for decades now. He and Mom rarely miss church, even in their eighties. They love God and seek to serve and obey him. As I write this he is fading from us—slowly but surely—because of dementia. I wish there was a drug that could "fix" this condition.

I know what some of you are thinking…

- What about God, His Word, prayer, and church?
- What did people do before the discovery of medication — back in biblical times up to the nineteenth century?

Your questions are valid. Allow me to introduce you to Bob Foster. Bob has helped not only me but thousands of people through Christian Counseling Associates here in Central Florida.

Tim: Bob, how long have you been counseling — and for our readers' understanding, what are your credentials?

Bob: I've been counseling for over thirty years, seven in pastoral counseling, twenty-four as a Florida licensed counselor. Thirty-one years ago, we opened Christian Counseling Associates here in Altamonte Springs, FL. And it's my joy to counsel.

Tim: That's a long time, thirty-plus years! In that time frame, how many people do you think you've seen? How many people have sat under your ministry, both in pastoral counseling and with CCA?

Bob: I've probably seen somewhere between 5,000 and 6,000 people of all ages and types; the very poor, very affluent, children, teens, white collar, blue collar, large church pastors, small church pastors. My greatest joy is working with pastors because I feel that if I help them, they can more effectively help their parishioners.

Tim: So you're saying, you've seen and continue to see many who are spiritual leaders in churches and non-profits? There are that many spiritual leaders in this type of need?

Bob: At CCA, we are actually seeing leaders of all types, but yes, many are spiritual leaders. One reason is, I think, because of the high levels of stress in our culture, and we know that stress depletes serotonin levels in our bodies, thus requiring, for many, medication to help supplement what is lost through stress. As well, some are just having what we call a "faith crisis" wondering where God is in all of their pain and loss.

Tim: Are you an advocate of using medication to help people battling depression?

Bob: Absolutely. If you have diabetes, you need insulin. If you have certain heart problems, you need appropriate medication. And many need medication to help them with their depression symptoms. Medication, in the short term, "stops the bleeding" emotionally. And while some may need medication for the short term, others will need medication longer, and some perhaps for life. One of my clients, an attorney in his fifties, had been in and out of counseling most of his adult life. A committed Christian, he had overturned every stone he could think of; attending seminars, memorizing and meditating on Scripture, research, small groups, etc. He was laboring under the suspicion that many deal with, such as "there must be some spiritual principle I am missing." In our third session, we discovered that there was a strong family history of depression. I referred him to a psychiatrist who prescribed medication for him; and in a month, his words were, "Bob I feel like I've come out of a fog. So this is how people live!"

Tim: You and I get that, but here's the question I know some are thinking. "Where is your faith?" and "What did the people in the Bible do with their depression, with their desperate situations? Shouldn't we just go to God and ask him to minister to our minds and emotions?" And what about what you referred to, a "crisis of faith"?

Bob: My first response would be that the people in the Bible suffered just like we all suffer. When we read the Psalms of David, for instance, and we see the emotional swings in that particular Psalm (e.g. Psalms 22, 69, 70), David is battling for his emotional equilibrium. We read of the emotional battles Jeremiah went through, and others. I can't help but think some of their pain might have been mitigated if they had had the advantage of modern medicine. Both men had a series of faith crises which is simply a wondering about where God is or what is He doing in a circumstance or loss, and a crisis of faith can be an emotional trigger that puts some over the edge, leading to prolonged times of depression. Also, I believe one of the answers to prayer for help is medication. In my experience, most of my patients who are on medication need it and continue to need it from a biological standpoint. Who was it that wrote the hymn, "There Is a Fountain Filled with Blood" who battled depression?

Tim: I believe you're referring to William Cowper (pronounced "Cooper")?

Bob: Yes, that's him. Here was a poor soul, as the story goes, who was so depressed that he was institutionalized for two to three years, he walked away from the faith for a period of time and returned when he heard one of his hymns being sung as he walked by a church. Even then, he battled depression all of his adult life. I'm quite sure medication could have helped him as well as the great English pastor, Charles Haddon Spurgeon, who battled depression and physical ailments so intensely, he would have to go away for months at a time for renewal and recuperation.

I once counseled a man who works for a Christian not-for-profit organization. His life was marked by one word: dread. As he drove to work in the morning (and mornings are usually the toughest time for us depressives), a feeling of foreboding fear would come over him. After a few hours of exploring his past and present, he was prescribed appropriate medication, and in three weeks his fear and dread were gone! You could sum up nine-tenths of his issue in one word: *biological*.

Tim: I remember after I had been under your care for some months, you made a guesstimate that helped me greatly. You said, "I think about sixty percent of your depression is biological, thirty percent is cognitive—how you are thinking about things, and ten percent is your diet, exercise and such. I may be off a little but not more than ten percent in any category. You have the medicinal help, and you eat pretty well and are starting to exercise. Where I can help you is the cognitive; how you think about things and process events, both past and present." Putting a number on it both relieved me and helped me to focus on where I needed to work.

Bob: When the scripture says that we are "fearfully and wonderfully made" (Psalm 139), it means we are intricate, complex, and, in our sin, complicated. When we come to the cross of Christ and ask for His forgiveness, often we forget to forgive ourselves...we don't really receive His forgiveness. So much of our past influences how we see our present. And if we don't think God is good, that God is our Redeemer, our Friend, and that He's a "healthy" Father; that He doesn't lose His temper, He doesn't rage, or if we simply see Him coming up short like an earthly father, our view of ourselves will be flawed and skewed. We will see God and everything else in a flawed and false way, based on what we've experienced in the past rather than seeing God, ourselves, and events on the basis of truth.

That's where the Bible comes in. It informs us of a perfect Father who loves without defect and always has us and our growth in grace high on His priority list. It tells us in Romans

8:28 that He is working everything together for the good of those who love Him and, get this...who are called (into relationship with Him) according to His purpose. Crazy as it sounds, even our sins and our depression can have redemptive purposes that God will use for His glory! If we begin to think in healthy ways, to process life on the basis of truth, our cognitive will inform our feelings. That's your thirty percent that you have to stay on top of.

By the way, how's that going?

Tim: Much better! I still have my days now and then but "down episodes" are becoming fewer in frequency and less debilitating, thankfully. I think I'm more in a healthy "maintenance mode" than a hard battle. But daily vigilance is still necessary.

Bob: Yes, it is. So keep fighting. And as you exercise your "cognitive truth muscles" you will gain strength, stamina, and see even more improvement.

Tim: I hear you. Bob, when we do give in to not fighting — when we do feel like giving up — guilt seems to, at times, be overwhelming. A sense of hopelessness, like, "I'll never get this right" or "What's the use of trying?" and "I just keep failing" are messages that seem to overtake us at times. What do we do with that?

Bob: Let's talk about guilt. First, what is it? Simply defined, it is a feeling of remorse or responsibility for having broken a rule or law. Since God has laws, and all of us at some point have broken His law, we are all guilty of breaking His law, which makes us...guilty. And if we are guilty, then we have punishment coming. But again, this is where the love of God and the cross of Jesus comes in. Christ takes the punishment for our guilt — all of it — on Himself and God punishes Him for our guiltiness. When we receive Him as our Savior, all of our guilt is credited to Him and all His goodness (the Bible calls it righteousness or literally, "rightness") is credited judicially to us!

Tim: I have still never gotten over that. All my sin is put on Him, and all His goodness is credited to me so I can be forgiven, free of guilt, love God and people, go to heaven, and appreciate life as it has always been meant to be, depression notwithstanding!

Bob: Exactly. And what does Romans 8:1 say? "There is therefore now no condemnation for those who are in Christ Jesus." This means we are no longer guilty! For the Christian, God moves from using "guilt" to using "conviction." And God is always specific. He will whisper to us, "Bob, that was an unkind word," or "I really wanted you to speak a word of encouragement to that stranger and you walked on by."

Tim: So why do we as Christians feel guilty?

Bob: For one, we may be guilty! But again, when we are guilty of breaking God's law, He brings conviction for correction, not condemnation. He does not put us down and He is specific regarding what we did or didn't do and what we need to do about it. He says, "My sheep hear My voice," and it is never ever condemning.

But we also have an enemy called the devil who has an agenda to accuse our consciences. And he always does it in generalities, never specifics. His tactic is to tear us down and to take us out:

- "If you were really a good Christian you wouldn't (think, talk, act) like that."
- "You are such a failure."
- "See? You just keep blowing it! You'll never win over this!"
- "See? No one likes you really; they just put up with you."
- "Uh huh...so you think you are a spiritual leader? Spiritual leaders don't..."

You get the idea.

Tim: Sounds like the tapes that I sometimes allow to play in my head. You know, the "you're not good enough and you'll never have enough," messages.

Bob: Exactly. And we have to battle those false accusations with truth. Again, seeing ourselves as God sees us in Christ — forgiven, redeemed, beloved, new, blessed, and full of what we call a "kingdom of God purpose" — is crucial.

Tim: Any other thoughts or insights on guilt, false or real?

Bob: I find it ironic that those who feel they are very guilty aren't as much as they think, and those who think they aren't, are! In general, the church has too much guilt, and the world, which has an entitlement obsession, doesn't have enough. But in my view, it's not our job to pronounce guilt, but to lovingly bring the Word of God into the conversation and let the Holy Spirit do what He does best, which is to "convict the world of guilt in regard to sin, and righteousness, and judgment" (John 16:8).

Tim: Bob, this has been helpful. What would be your advice to someone looking for the right counselor to help them through a time of depression?

Bob: First, they could call several large local churches, some of which have licensed counselors on staff. They can usually recommend two or three very competent counselors to begin the process. One can also contact Focus on the Family in Colorado Springs, Colorado. They have a national network of counselors they recommend for different areas of the country.

Tim: Any final words?

Bob: Yes. God wants you, dear reader, to know Him more than you want to know Him. Come to Him with all of your pain and He will help you hope again. We and others in the helping profession are here for you. It's what we do and it's always an honor to be of service. God bless you.

CHAPTER 14

AVOIDING DISSONANCE AND DEFEAT

*"The great triad of enemies for Christian growth
contain the world, the flesh, and the devil."*
—R. C. Sproul[44]

In times of war, various battle cries have been heard and
made famous:

- "Battle stations! Battle stations!"
- "To arms men! To arms!"
- "Remember the Alamo!"
- "Give me liberty or give me death!"
- "Tora, Tora, Tora!"
- "The Sword of the Lord and of Gideon!"[45]

Each of them is a rallying cry to inspire men to not lose
heart and to fight with all their might! The cry helps to steel
the nerves and bolster faltering courage because the chance is
real that one may not come back alive.

To not include this last chapter would be an incomplete
overview of depression. To not discuss spiritual warfare with
more specificity than in chapter five would be a disservice to
you, my reader and friend. The battle is real, and it may or
may not play a part in your struggle with depression.

It did in mine, big time, especially in depression #2.

Let's remember that our country's military goes to war on
three primary fronts:

- Land (Army, Marines)
- Sea (Navy, Coast Guard)
- Air (Air Force)

One type of battle uses ground troops. Another employs ships and submarines. Finally, fighter jets take control of the skies. And the battle will go best when all three are in communication and concert with one another.

In depression, we also fight on three fronts: the world, the flesh, and the devil — these can contribute to depression.

> *Do not love the world or the things in the world. If anyone loves the world, the love of the Father is not in him. For all that is in the world — the desires of the flesh and the desires of the eyes and pride of life — is not from the Father but is from the world. And the world is passing away along with its desires, but whoever does the will of God abides forever* (1 John 2:15-17, ESV).

These verses describe the first two of our three battlefronts.

1. The World

New Testament Greek has three words for *world,* and in these verses, the word is *cosmos.* Here it means "the world-system" or "the way of the world," in contrast to God's way. This is a man-centered world-view, rather than biblical or theocentric. Every day the world, primarily through media, influences us with its way of thinking, seeing, and doing.

A perfect example is the abortion issue. The world tells us:

- The baby is a blob of tissue or sometimes called a "fetus" (technically correct but the term tends to dehumanize a child in the womb made in the image of God).
- A woman has the exclusive right to choose life or death for the baby because her body and her rights take precedence.
- We need abortion for population control.

But in truth, the world's way is in stark contrast with a biblical or theocentric view of life (see Psalms 139:13–16, Jeremiah 1:4–5, Luke 1:31, 39–45).

God says, *"For My thoughts are not your thoughts, neither are your ways My ways."* Also: *"As the heavens are higher than the earth, so are My ways higher than your ways and My thoughts than your thoughts"* (Isaiah 55:8–9).

Back in the early 1990s, we experienced a hailstorm in Central Florida. The insurance adjuster came out to assess our roof and we received a $4,500 check to replace the roof.

I went up on the roof and saw (with my untrained eye) very little damage. I thought, "Ha! I don't have to fix this. I can use that money for some other things."

I bragged to two friends and my dad that I would get to rip off the insurance company. I had forgotten that Dad was an insurance adjuster.

Dad did not confront me; he just said, "Well, there's probably some damage there that you didn't see." He left it at that.

I think it was his way of saying, "Son

- don't be dumb,
- don't be deceived, and
- don't be deceptive."

And God was saying, "Be smart and be ethical." I got the new roof. I had been thinking from a flawed worldview — get what you can now and worry about the consequences later.

Mankind's way — the way of the world — stands most often in competition with God and His ways. So we must engage this battle with our own thinking and way of seeing things. We do this through God's Word and other good books that explain, with clarity and detail, the Christian worldview.[46]

2. The Flesh

The Greek word *sarx*, that translates to *flesh* in 1 John 2:16, has several definitions. In this context, it means, "the seat of sin in man"⁴⁷ and, "the lower and temporary element in the Christian."⁴⁸

This battle is with *me*! This is about what I think and do—or don't think and don't do. It's how I treat people and communicate. The enemies are me, myself, and I.

The flesh, that part of me that wants control, is my battle with myself. It is me attempting to live, either through rebellion or neglect, apart from God and rely on myself to improve morally, spiritually, or emotionally. For a closer look at "we the flesh," see Galatians 5:19–21:

> *When you follow the desires of your sinful nature, the results are very clear: sexual immorality, impurity, lustful pleasures, idolatry, sorcery, hostility, quarreling, jealousy, outbursts of anger, selfish ambition, dissension, division, envy, drunkenness, wild parties, and other sins like these. Let me tell you again, as I have before, that anyone living that sort of life will not inherit the Kingdom of God* (NLT).

That is quite a list. And when I engage in any of those sinful activities, I let people down—my family, my friends, and those God has called me to serve. Not to mention myself and God.

And this can be depressing. Yes, sin can be a cause of depression. Notice I said a cause. For some, it may be the primary cause in the absence of medical or chemical issues. Your sinful behavior could very well be just sinful rebellion of the heart. And that is a spiritual condition that affects your emotional condition.

Whether your behavior is a cause or effect of your depression, your responsibility is to reach out and ask for help. You need to become accountable to a friend or counselor and manage your behavior the best you can at the time. Again, part of your behavior is to ask for help.

I remember arriving at my hotel on a typical Saturday evening before a Sunday of concerts and speaking. I turned on ESPN to hear about the upcoming George Forman fight on HBO at 9 p.m. I thought, "Great! I'll go over my program for tomorrow, get some room service, and watch the fight!" That went well until about the fifth round when a promo aired for a sexy and provocative film to follow the fight. Suddenly, I wanted to watch that film. But I didn't want to—except the "want to watch" was growing in strength. And then, irrespective of Forman, a fight was on that really mattered.

I knew I was going down without help. I phoned Mike in Dallas and gave him the details.

He began to ask me questions like, "If you watch this film, will you sin against your wife and kids? Will you violate the vows you took on your wedding day? Tomorrow will you be able to sing and teach God's word with integrity?"

We prayed together, and guess what? When the call ended, the temptation was gone.

I must add one of the last things Mike said: "Now, Tim, I'm going to call you in fifteen minutes...or ten...or I may not call at all. But you don't know, do you?" We laughed, said goodnight, and hung up. He called about twenty minutes later and I was almost asleep.

These two areas, the world (system) and the flesh (sinful propensity), require much vigilance. They are tough to battle with and against. But the third front will require a bit more understanding to fight successfully.

3. The Devil

Be alert and of sober mind. Your enemy the devil prowls around like a roaring lion looking for someone to devour. Resist him, standing firm in the faith, because you know that the family of believers throughout the world is undergoing the same kind of sufferings (1 Peter 5:8–9).

Spiritual warfare is a misunderstood topic today. Thankfully, I can refer you to some helpful books in the bibliography. A short overview will get you going.

Before God created man, He created angelic beings. Lucifer was one of His lead angels, along with Michael and Gabriel. Jealousy and pride took root in Lucifer's heart, and he led a rebellion against God. One-third of the angels defected with him, and they became "fallen angels" or demons because they sinned. God kicked them out of heaven.

Ever since Eden, Satan and his demons have led a full-on assault against humanity. Satan hates God and His entire creation, but especially humanity. After all, we are made "in the image of God." The Bible calls Satan

- a liar (John 8:44).
- a dragon (Revelation 12:3–9).
- a serpent (Revelation 12:3–9).
- a "murderer from the beginning" (John 8:44).
- the accuser of the people of God (Revelation 12:10).
- an angel of light (deception, 2 Corinthians 11:14).
- the adversary (1 Peter 5:8).
- the "father of lies" (John 8:44).
- the tempter (Matthew 4:3; 1 Thessalonians 3:5).
- the thief (John 10:10).
- the wicked one (1 John 2:13–14).
- the evil one (John 17:15).

This is only a partial list, but it gives you an idea of whom and what we battle. Satan and his demons use primarily intimidation, distraction, deception, and discouragement to lead people further away from God and closer to the kingdom of darkness.

My first head-to-head encounter with a demon came in September of 1976. I was traveling with the Word of Life musical drama presentation Let Freedom Ring. We had toured fourteen cities in the spring and filmed a one-hour television special to air in December. Through the fall, we were to perform in another fifty or so cities in the eastern U.S.

The night before opening in Pittsburg, we stayed in Hamburg, New York. My roommate and I hit the sack around midnight, but soon I was half awake. Suddenly, I felt a something—a being, whatever—physically pressing me into the mattress. My body vibrated with an electric current pulsing through me! I tried to wrestle free, but the pressure only increased.

A fear I'd never known gripped me, and then BAM! A blinding light bathed me for what had to be no more than five seconds and then—peace. Quiet. Absolute tranquility.

Still shaking from the experience, I called to my roommate who had slept through the whole event. I shared what happened; thankfully, he did not dismiss me as crazy.

I contend that attack was a demon trying to intimidate me from presenting the gospel at my best. Then I was rescued by a true angel of light.

I had additional encounters for the next eighteen years as I learned to do battle by applying God's word accurately and surgically. I also had to close some doors that invited the activity of the enemy into my life. My last direct confrontation with demonic activity ended in 1994, to the praise of our God and Savior, King Jesus!

What happened in those encounters? The enemy used scare tactics. He frustrated ministry plans. He worked against my marriage and finances. On two specific occasions, he even attacked my infant son, Ivan. The Bible says Satan is a lying thief who only comes to "steal, kill, and destroy" (John 10:10) everything good, godly, and holy.

He attacks the depressive by accusation—leading to discouragement and discontentment (lack of contentment is most often a sin unless it is a motivation for improvement). Remember my recordings of "not good enough, never have enough"? He has used these cunningly in my mind over the years. Remember, he comes to steal, kill, and destroy. He first steals your joy and purpose, which can kill motivation and hope. Finally he seeks to lead you to become ineffective through disengagement. If he's successful in that, he can push you to suicide.

But you need not fear. You can fight on these three fronts for your soul.

Finally, be strong in the Lord and in his mighty power. Put on the full armor of God, so that you can take your stand against the devil's schemes. For our struggle is not against flesh and blood, but against the rulers, against the authorities, against the powers of this dark world and against the spiritual forces of evil in the heavenly realms. Therefore put on the full armor of God, so that when the day of evil comes, you may be able to stand your ground, and after you have done everything, to stand. Stand firm then, with the belt of truth buckled around your waist, with the breastplate of righteousness in place, and with your feet fitted with the readiness that comes from the gospel of peace. In addition to all this, take up the shield of faith, with which you can extinguish all the flaming arrows of the evil one. Take the helmet of salvation and the sword of the Spirit, which is the word of God. And pray in the Spirit on all occasions with all kinds of prayers and requests. With this in mind, be alert and always keep on praying for all the Lord's people (Ephesians 6:10–18).

1. **The Belt of Truth.** Just as you get dressed in the morning, you must dress yourself spiritually for battle. Your center of gravity is your core, your midsection. What does the belt do in a Roman suit of armor? It fastens the other pieces in their places as the foundation for the armor. You must claim truth to battle the enemy's lies. The core of your thinking must have grounding in truth. When my kids call my wife for prayer, her declaration of truth is: "I thank you that I am blessed, chosen, adopted, accepted, redeemed, and forgiven." One of my daughters says that hearing these words aloud in the midst of anxiety is an instant calm to her soul, regardless of the storm within.

AVOIDING DISSONANCE AND DEFEAT

2. **The Breastplate of Righteousness**. The breastplate protects the vital organs, and so does righteousness (*"Above all else, guard your heart, for everything you do flows from it"* — Proverbs 4:23). You must pursue righteousness actively within your lifestyle. You must fulfill Christ's command to be holy and set apart. When you engage in things of the world, you cheapen the righteous blood meant to cover you. Conversely, when you actively pursue righteousness and make it a conscious part of your daily walk, you protect your heart — your most vital part — from evil.

3. **Feet Fitted with the Gospel of Peace**. The Roman soldier wore a boot with small spikes (much like athletic cleats today) to stand his ground in slippery places. You must be a sure-footed warrior against evil. When you are at peace with God (Romans 5:1) and are experiencing the peace of God (Philippians 4:7), you will rarely get knocked off your spiritual feet. You can stand firmly on the gospel of peace — the death, burial, and resurrection of Jesus Christ (2 Corinthians 15:1–4).

4. **The Shield of Faith**. Roman infantrymen had two shields; a small one for protection in hand-to-hand combat and the large *thureos* (thoo-reh-os' from the Greek word for door, *thura*) shield that protected the entire body. On the front, it had six layers of animal skins that would absorb the fiery arrows of enemy combatants. This shield enabled the Roman soldier to advance through a hail of arrows! The metaphor is quite encouraging, wouldn't you say? When the enemy hurls accusations, guilt, condemnation, and discouragement, you can lift the shield of faith and not only not take the hit, but actually quench these fiery arrows.

5. **The Helmet of Salvation**. The helmet protects your mind. Read this amazing verse, 1 Corinthians 2:16 —

"We have the mind of Christ." Satan will do anything to disrupt your clear thinking in Christ. Listen to the words of Pastor John MacArthur: "The fact that the helmet is related to salvation indicates that Satan's blows are directed at the believer's security and assurance in Christ. The two dangerous edges of Satan's spiritual broadsword are discouragement and doubt. To discourage us he points to our failures, our sins, our unresolved problems, our poor health, or to whatever else seems negative in our lives in order to make us lose confidence in the love and care of our heavenly Father."[49]

You must focus on the facts that you have been saved from the *penalty* of your sins, that you are being saved from the *power* of sin, and someday (Yes!) you will with finality be saved from the *presence* of sin. As you embrace this truth you will experience what the writer to the Hebrews calls "so great salvation" (Hebrews 2:3, KJV).

6. **The Sword of the Spirit**. Our only offensive weapon is Jesus Himself — the Word inscribed, the Scriptures, and the Word Incarnate. He is the true logos (word). Many tools will help fortify us, as discussed in chapter six, but the ultimate weapon is Scripture. Psalms 119:11 says, "I have hidden Your word in my heart that I might not sin against You." When Jesus confronted Satan in Matthew 4, he repeatedly quoted the Word of God, the Sword of the Spirit, to defeat his enemy. That's why Scripture memory — having the Word of God ready on your tongue — is like a spiritual sword that you use against temptation.

7. **Spirit-Filled Prayer**. The warrior of the Lord will respond to these designations in the text:

    a. The *when* of prayer — "on all occasions...always"

b. The *what* of prayer—"all kinds of prayers and requests"
c. The *who* of prayer—"all the Lord's people"

We are in a battle for ourselves and for others in the Lord's army. We pray often and always (meaning, ready at any time for any reason). We pray prayers of praise, thanksgiving, intercession, supplication, requests, and worship. We do so for the Lord's people. This doesn't mean you shouldn't pray for lost people or the needs of the world. However, in warfare prayer, you concentrate on the needs of yourself and fellow troops on the battlefront and support personnel behind the scenes.

These dimensions of spiritual readiness come to you by the salvation you have in Christ. As you exercise these weapons (not toys or tools) in faith, you become experientially what the Bible calls:

1. Conquerors (Romans 8:37) and
2. Overcomers (I John 4:4; 5:4)

And they overcame him by the blood of the Lamb, and by the word of their testimony; and they loved not their lives unto the death (Revelation 12:11, KJV).

Whether you fight the world, the flesh or the devil (or all three at the same time), your battle is to engage and rely on the strength of the Lord in the fray. You do that best not as an isolated sniper but by going on patrol with fellow soldiers—others on the same journey who understand the stakes and the call to become conquerors for His kingdom's sake.

Do not go it alone when you do not have to. Mike was there for me at a critical time in that hotel room. The Father provides what you need, and one of the provisions is fellow fighters. Reach out to them, for their sake as well as yours. You will be less depressed and more effective.

Though one may be overpowered, two can defend themselves. A cord of three strands is not quickly broken (Ecclesiastes 4:12).

CONCLUSION

S ome may read this book and surmise that I think all one needs to do is read and study Scripture more, pray more, get some good counseling, be in community and *voilà!* – you can overcome depression!

I believe that is true for many, even most who simply struggle with the blues, down times or mild depression. As I have shared, it was a part of my healing. But medication and cognitive therapy were critical (and continue to be) major factors in my *ongoing* healing with clinical depression.

But what about others whose struggle is much deeper? What about some of you who may have an eighty to ninety percent chemical factor? What about those who have to be hospitalized or, here in Florida, "Baker-Acted" (the Florida Mental Health Act of 1971 that allows for the involuntary institutionalization of persons who are a danger to themselves and/or others)?

I have a friend who is godly, has written discipleship curriculum, been a church leader and loves God with all her heart…who had to be institutionalized. She was not in sin. She battles mental illness and is currently "fine" having gotten the right medication and help. Could it happen again? Yes, unfortunately.

As I have shared my pre-published manuscript with several friends, the stories just continue to come in; stories of friends, acquaintances, and family members who struggle with different types of depression:

- A committed regional Christian recording artist with a fruitful ministry took his life.
- A pastor's wife had to be hospitalized, her clinical depression is so debilitating. I know her personally; she loves God with all her heart but is in the fight for her life.
- A former missionary shared her story of how she has battled depression all her adult life but felt she had to

SINGING HALLELUJAH WHEN YOU FEEL LIKE HELL

keep it secret due to how those in the church would view her.

But no matter where you are on the spectrum of mental illness, from an occasional day or week of the blues to severe clinical depression, time with the Lord can only help. It's like leadership guru Zig Ziglar once said, "I can think positively all I want and it won't make me an NFL quarterback. But whatever I do, positivity will only help me." Likewise, reading God's word, prayer, fellowship with like-minded fellow-strugglers, and good books will help anyone and everyone. These are the basics of the Christian life and we all need that God-connection, whatever our personal situation.

You will note that throughout this book I've often used the word *journey*. That was intentional because it's exactly what we all are on—a journey. I wish overcoming depression and our "issues" wasn't such a protracted and involved process for most of us. I wish it was sooner than later. But then, I also wish my sanctification (growing in spiritual maturity) didn't take so long. It's like the guy with the cigar in the old Hertz commercial who grumbles, "I hate to wait!" Yeah, that's most of us.

However, it seems that our Heavenly Father is quite content to take His time bringing all of us to where *He* wants us, on *His* timetable—rather than where we think we'd rather be on *our* timetable. After many years I'm learning that God is good. He is gracious, and…He is patient.

He has cut us a lot of slack. So cut yourself some and extend it to others as well. Engage in the process and walk with Him. Take advantage of the tools and resources in this book and the others that you'll encounter along the way. Journey on, seeking to walk not only *with* Him, but *like* Him as well.

And the God of all grace, who called you to his eternal glory in Christ, after you have suffered a little while, will himself restore you and make you strong, firm and steadfast. To him be the power for ever and ever. Amen (I Peter 5:10–11

A WORD ABOUT HELL

In our culture we use the word *hell*

1. as an exclamation: "What the hell was that?!"
2. as a pejorative: "Go to hell!"
3. as a congratulatory: "That was a hell of a game you played!
4. as a descriptive: "I feel like hell today."

Number four is *almost* how I've chosen to use it in the book title *Singing Hallelujah When You Feel Like Hell*. There is a fifth usage of the word and that is theological.

Why do we use the word *hell* in these ways? Where did the term come from?

THE GARDEN

When God created Adam and Eve (Genesis chapters 1 and 2) they were created because they were wanted. God was not lonely, He was creating us to know Him for who He is and to give us the joy of living life to its intended abundance (see John 10:10). He wanted a people who would be fulfilled in every way. He would come walking in the "cool of the day" (Genesis 3:8) looking for them to simply hang out. And God is looking for you too!

In any relationship there are rules. With our spouses we have unwritten rules and expectations. When those are broken it hurts relationship. Likewise, there are rules we have with our children and even friends. It's just part of relationship. When Adam and Eve broke God's rule and ate the forbidden fruit (sinned) Paradise was lost. The sweet relationship was broken and we've been living with "hell on earth" ever since. Hell, both literally and metaphorically, is everything heaven isn't. And we have come to use the term to describe something undesirable, frustrating or even direct it toward someone we don't like or disagree with.

GOOD NEWS!

Remembering that God first created us for Himself and for us to know Him in all His wonder, we now know why Jesus came to die for us: to restore us to the intended purpose God first had; paradise and fellowship with Him for eternity!

Enter Jesus: *"For God so loved the world that He gave His only begotten Son, that whoever believes in Him should not perish but have everlasting life."* [50]

To rescue and restore us God sent His Son Jesus so that we could live in abundance here on earth experiencing His assistance, help, encouragement, balm, hope, and strength and live with Him in heaven forever. Jesus made that possible when He went to a cruel crucifixion, was buried and then rose from the dead three days later.

> *For Christ also suffered once for sins, the righteous for the unrighteous, to bring you to God.* [51]

I love that phrase, "to bring you to God."

Friend, God loves you and wants a relationship with you. It can be yours. It's a free gift.

> *For it is by grace you have been saved, through faith – and this is not from yourselves, it is the gift of God, not by works, so that no one can boast.* [52]

To begin a life of restoration, purpose, meaning, overcoming and abundance, I invite you to pray a prayer like the one I prayed years ago:

> *Dear God in heaven, I admit that I am living life on my own and need you in my life. I have broken Your laws of right and wrong. But I believe that you gave Your Son, Jesus Christ, God in the flesh, to die for my sins. I believe*

that He rose from the dead to guarantee that I can experience your love and live with you forever. By faith I receive Your grace to me. Amen.

If you prayed that prayer, I'd like to send you a free PDF I've written entitled, "I Prayed That Prayer...What Now?" Contact me at TimKaufman.com and I'll email it your way.

Welcome to God's family!

ADDENDUM 2
A SOBER WORD OF CAUTION

Antidepressant medications carry warning labels for a reason.

October 24, 2015 will be a day the friends and family of Warren and Ellie Jenkins will never forget.

I first met Warren and Ellie when I was a freshman in college. Warren was a senior but when Ellie arrived on our campus as a freshman he swooped in quickly to win her heart before anyone else had a chance! They married the summer of 1972 and took up residence in northern Virginia, assisting as strong lay people to plant a church and became involved in helping students, missionaries, and raising a godly family. They were the prototypical American Christian family who lived to serve and help others. As a Christian school teacher, I was grateful for the summer job Warren and his brother Russ gave me in 1981 to help bridge my income until school resumed in the fall.

But the Jenkins' world was rocked on that fateful October day when Ellie ended her life.

Ellie began to experience anxiety in 2008 due to menopause. According to Warren and their daughter Heather, a registered nurse, doctors were pretty successful in helping Ellie manage her ups and downs with a combination of hormone replacement therapy and antidepressants.

All seemed well until 2014 when Ellie's anxiety returned following a hysterectomy. This time a stronger drug combination was tried with side effects. Though experimentation continued, the medications were actually making Ellie's depression worse and she was losing her battle with the drug induced suicidal thoughts...to the point where Ellie attempted to take her life in October of 2014, thankfully, unsuccessfully.

This was not the Ellie that I nor anyone knew.

Ellie's recovery seemed good as she was grateful that she was not able to take her life. She even wrote a six-page testimonial of how God had brought her through this ordeal.

But a mere six months later she was battling again. New medications were tried, doses increased and all to no avail. Her reactions to the medications were again increasing her depression and accompanying suicidal thoughts. Ellie lost hope and took her life almost a year to the day she had attempted it the first time.

Warren and his family have allowed me to share their story for two reasons:

1. To help bring balance to Chapter 13 and a word of caution to you, dear reader, to make sure you are in close and accountable constant contact with your doctor(s), family members and friends. Life does not have to end for you as it did Ellie.

2. To be redemptive. Warren said to me, "We want people to know that Ellie loved the Lord, was a wonderful wife, mother, and grandmother, and this can happen to anyone! We want the Lord to use our story in whatever way it can be used to help others."

SUGGESTED READING

Remember to ask the Father for the right book at the right time. It may not be on this list. All books listed can be found (to date) at www.Amazon.com/books.

A Few Things I've Learned Since I Knew It All by Jerry Cook

A Tale of Three Kings by Gene Edwards

Abba's Child by Brennan Manning

Balancing the Christian Life by Charles Ryrie

Battlefield for the Mind by Joyce Meyer

Boundaries by Henry Cloud and John Townsend

Breaking Strongholds by Thomas B. White

Disappointment with God by Philip Yancey

Healing for Damaged Emotions by David Seamands

Healing of Memories by David Seamands

Healing the Hurts of Your Past by F. Remy Diederich

How to Win Friends and Influence People by Dale Carnegie

Inside Out by Larry Crabb

Overcoming the Adversary by Mark Bubeck

People of the Lie by M. Scott Peck

Ruthless Trust by Brennan Manning

Safe People by Henry Cloud and John Townsend

Secrets of Your Family Tree by Cloud and Townsend (and others)

Skill with People by Les Giblin

The Adversary by Mark Bubeck

The Believer's Guide to Spiritual Warfare by Thomas B. White

The Bondage Breaker by Neil Anderson

The Bondage Breaker: The Next Step by Neil Anderson

The Gift of Pain by Philip Yancey and Dr. Paul Brand

The Jesus I Never Knew by Philip Yancey

The Journey of Desire by John Eldredge

The Normal Christian Life by Watchman Nee

The Question That Never Goes Away by Philip Yancey

The Ragamuffin Gospel by Brennan Manning

The Sacred Romance by John Eldredge

The Screwtape Letters by C. S. Lewis

The Wisdom of Tenderness by Brennan Manning

Understanding People by Larry Crabb

Victory Over the Darkness by Neil Anderson

Waking the Dead by John Eldredge

Walking with God Through Pain & Suffering by Timothy Keller

What's So Amazing About Grace by Philip Yancey

Where is God When it Hurts by Philip Yancey

Wild at Heart by John Eldredge

ABOUT THE AUTHOR

T im Kaufman is an international gospel music artist with eleven vocal albums to his credit. He is a speaker, teacher, publisher, and songwriter, but best of all, a husband, father, and grandfather. Tim and Alicia have five adult children, three sons-in-law, and a grand-girl named Piper.

Tim can be contacted at www.TimKaufman.com

ENDNOTES

¹ http://www.dictionary.com/browse/depression?s=t

² http://www.webmd.com/depression/guide/causes-depression,
   WebMD Medical Reference

View Article Sources

SOURCES:

National Institute of Mental Health: "Causes of Depression" and "What
   is Depression?"
SAMSHA's National Mental Health Information Center: "Mood
   Disorders."
American Psychiatric Association. *Diagnostic and Statistical Manual of
   Mental Disorders: DSM-IV-TR,* American Psychiatric Pub, 2000.
Fieve, R. Bipolar II, Rodale Books, 2006.

Reviewed by Joseph Goldberg, MD on February 27, 2016
© 2016 WebMD, LLC. All rights reserved.

³ http://www.medicaldaily.com/am-i-depressed-types-people-more-
   prone-depression-299286

⁴ ibid.

⁵ ibid.

⁶ http://ajp.psychiatryonline.org/doi/abs/10.1176/appi.ajp.157.10.1552

⁷ http://www.dictionary.com/browse/serotonin?s=t

⁸ https://www.neurogistics.com/TheScience/
   WhatareNeurotransmi09CE.asp

⁹ ibid.

¹⁰ Pam Rosewell Moore, *Life Lessons From the Hiding Place,* Chosen Books
   (a div. of Baker Publishing Group, Grand Rapids, MI) 2004, pp. 125–
   126.

¹¹ http://www.strengthsfinder.com/home.aspx

¹² See Judges 6:36–40

[13] These components are necessary in any range of depression, from mild to severe although the identification and/or realization of goals, purpose and meaning may not be until a season of healing and recovery takes place.

[14] http://www.merriam-webster.com/dictionary/repression

[15] http://harvardmagazine.com/2008/01/repressed-memory.html

[16] https://faculty.washington.edu/eloftus/Articles/lof93.htm

[17] http://biblehub.com/greek/3794.htm

[18] ibid.

[19] http://www.renner.org/strongholds/two-kinds-of-strongholds/

[20] Alexander MacLaren, http://biblehub.com/commentaries/mark/8-22.htm

[21] From the song "He Will Provide" by Tim Kaufman and Steve Rogers, © Tim Kaufman Ministries, Inc., 1999. All rights reserved.

[22] Philippians 2:13

[23] Hebrews 2:11

[24] The Levites were the one tribe of God that was not given an inheritance in the land of Israel but were to live off of the provisions of the other 12 tribes. They were to focus solely on the sacrificial and worship system for the nation. They were called to lead the people of God without worldly distractions. "The Levites have no share or inheritance among their brothers; the Lord is their inheritance." (Deuteronomy 10:9).

[25] From the song "He Will Provide" by Tim Kaufman and Steve Rogers, © Tim Kaufman Ministries, Inc., 1999. All rights reserved.

[26] Joyce Meyer, *Battlefield For the Mind*, Harrison House, (Tulsa, OK), p. 61.

[27] http://www.businessnewsdaily.com/2381-albert-einstein-business-tips.html

[28] http://brownbackmason.com/articles/10-principles-of-cognitive-behavioral-therapy-cbt

[29] http://www.uncommonhelp.me/articles/stop-self-sabotage-behaviour/

30 https://www.goodreads.com/author/quotes/162578.Bren_Brown

31 http://www.goodreads.com/quotes/tag/isolation

32 http://www.charismanews.com/opinion/watchman-on-the-wall/42063-why-are-so-many-pastors-committing-suicide

33 http://thomrainer.com/2014/04/eight-struggles-pastors-face-rainer-leadership-050/

34 http://www.pastorburnout.com/pastor-burnout-statistics.html

35 ibid.

36 https://today.duke.edu/2013/08/clergydepressionnewsrelease

37 http://www.christianity.com/blogs/dr-james-emery-white/a-pastors-hide.html

38 http://www.everydayhealth.com/hs/major-depression/depression-statistics/

39 http://www.webmd.com/depression/features/depression-traps-and-pitfalls#1

40 http://www.inc.com/dave-kerpen/15-quotes-to-inspire-great-team-work.html

41 http://www.imdb.com/title/tt0113483/

42 http://www.goodreads.com/quotes/tag/counseling

43 http://www.goodtherapy.org/blog/myth-madness-going-to-therapy-means-im-weak-flawed-or-crazy-1007137

44 http://www.azquotes.com/quote/867505

45 Judges 7:20

46 For a list of some of the top books on the Christian worldview, go to http://www.heartsandmindsbooks.com/booknotes/top_ten_books_on_a_christian_w/

47 *Vine's Expository Dictionary of New Testament Words*, W.E. Vine, M.A., 1940. Public Domain

48 ibid.

49 http://www.gty.org/resources/bible-qna/BQ060513/what-is-the-helmet-of-salvation

[50] John 3:16 (NKJV)

[51] 1 Peter 3:18

[52] Ephesians 2:8-9

Made in the USA
San Bernardino, CA
12 April 2017